ANGLICAN SPIRITUAL DIRECTION

Anglican Spiritual Direction

Peter Ball

COWLEY PUBLICATIONS
Cambridge ✦ Boston
Massachusetts

Library of Congress Cataloging in Publication Data:
Ball, Peter.
    Anglican spiritual direction/Peter Ball.
        p.   cm.
    Includes bibliographic references.
    ISBN 1-56101-159-2 (alk. paper)
    1. Spiritual direction. 2. Church of England—Doctrines. 3. Anglican Communion—Doctrines. I. Title.
BV5053.B35 1998
253.5′3′08823—DC21   98-26793
                                                                        CIP

Editor: Cynthia Shattuck
Cover Design: Vicki Black
Cover Art: *Solitary House* by Piet Mondrian (1898-1900).

This book is printed on recycled, acid-free paper and was produced in the United States of America.

Cowley Publications • 28 Temple Place
Boston, Massachusetts 02111
1-800-225-1534 • http://www.cowley.org

For Angela,
beloved wife, helper, and friend

He showed me the river of the water of life, sparkling like crystal, flowing out of the throne of God and the Lamb....On either side of the river stood a tree of life.... The leaves of the trees are for the healing of the nations.

(Revelation 22:1-2)

CONTENTS

Acknowledgments

No book on anything to do with the Christian life can claim to be original. I have to open this one by expressing my indebtedness to many people. It is the story of a tradition and there are hundreds of men and women, known and unknown, who have contributed to that tradition.

Among those who have guided me on my journey as a Christian and a priest I give thanks for Mark Hodson and John Eastaugh, under whom I trained as a curate at All Saints, Poplar. Father Charles Preston SSF, Reginald Somerset Ward, Norman Goodacre, and Alan Harrison have in turn accompanied me with spiritual counsel, while Elizabeth Smyth RC gave me immense encouragement and accurate criticism in my work as a director until her early death.

Then in the mutuality of spiritual direction I owe an immeasurable amount to those men and women who have trusted me with their confidence as a companion and guide on their journey. I thank them.

What follows in the book is a kind of anthology. I have received generous help from a large number of people to whom I turned for advice, information, and criticism. They include Donald Allchin, Raymond Avent, Brother Bernard SSF, Richard Buck, Tony Bryer (to whom I am particularly indebted for the generous loan of his research material on the Somerset Ward papers), Sister Denzil CSA, Laura Eastaugh, Sister Edna Monica SLG, David Gillett, Norman Goodacre, Richard Hayes, Sister Hilary CSMV, Gordon Jeff,

Kenneth Leech, Christopher Lowe, John Pearce, David Ritchie, David Smith, John Townroe, and Michael Vasey.

In preparing this present book for publication in America my thanks go to Dean Guy Lytle of The School of Theology at the University of the South at Sewanee, Tennessee, for the generous invitation to spend time there as a Fellow in Residence. I value the welcome and help given by members of the faculty and students there, with particular thanks to Bob Hughes, Tom Ward, Jim Dunkly, and the staff of the university library. While I was in America it was good to be able to spend time with Margaret Guenther at The General Seminary in New York, Martin Smith SSJE and Paul Wessenger SSJE at the monastery in Boston, Tilden Edwards at the Shalem Institute, Alan Jones, who by happy chance was visiting Nashville, and Sister Lucy and the Community of St. Mary at Sewanee. To them and many others I am most grateful for their time and interest.

An earlier version of this book was published by Mowbray in 1995 under the title *Journey into Truth*, and I am grateful for the publisher's willingness to allow me to develop a new American version. Much of the evidence for the tradition is to be found in quotations. Wherever possible I have given the reference to the source from which I have quoted and must apologize for any inaccuracy or omission. As a compulsive checker of footnotes myself, I think it would be helpful to assure the reader that the notes at the end of each chapter simply contain the references to the passages in the text. No other interesting information is hidden away there.

Chapter 1

By Way of Introduction

S trong religious experiences do not feature as a large part of my life. When they come, they are often associated with some place or event. For instance, going into York Minster brings me almost to tears with the beauty of its space and sense of holiness. I was also deeply moved by taking part in the ordinations of women friends to the priesthood, particularly when I had been involved as their companion on the long journey to that day.

The memory which fits best with the theme of this book comes from May 1987, when a group of us from England were members of a European conference at Gazzada, north of Milan. The theme was adult Christians coming to faith and baptism through the catechumenate. It was the year when the church celebrated the sixteen hundredth anniversary of the baptism of St. Augustine by St. Ambrose, Bishop of Milan. With the help of Ambrose, Augustine had come to the point where he was able to make a commitment to the Christian faith and to living a Christian life. Before going out to Gazzada, a town not far from the farm where Augustine went for a time of retreat before his baptism, we made a visit to the cathedral in Milan. In the excavations under what is now the Piazza del Duomo, we stood by the remains of the fourth-century baptistery where Ambrose and Augustine had stood sixteen centuries before.

The sense of continuity was overwhelming. My roots in the faith seemed to stretch so deep.

The relationship between these two people, one accompanying the other into deeper faith and fuller response to God, is our experience in spiritual direction today. In my work of helping people come to and grow in the Christian faith I am continually struck by the way God works through ordinary personal relationships. Family members, friends and friends of friends, and even people you hardly know seem to be used to raise awareness of God and his love and to trigger a response. Occasionally it is some clear teaching or advice given by the Christian friend that has this effect; more often it is something far less tangible. There is something about them—their character, the way they accept you, the way they give you space, the sense of respect and value you receive from them. It is the experience in one way or another of being loved for who you are.

Recognizing the importance of this truth reinforces for me all that spiritual direction stands for. It is essentially a relationship in which God is at work using one person to help another on the journey of faith. There are infinite varieties in the way it happens, from the very simplest everyday chatting between friends who would never think to describe their conversation by such a grand title, to formal sessions of spiritual counsel with someone who is skilled in this ministry.

My book is designed to give a picture of what this kind of relationship has meant to Anglicans over the centuries and what it means for us today in the Anglican Communion. It is meant to celebrate and also to encourage: celebrate the gifts with which God has blessed us and encourage men and women to use those gifts. I also hope to be able to give some feeling of the spiritual ethos of our church and to show some of the features that distinguish it from other traditions, focusing first on spiritual direction in the Church of England and then on its more recent flourishing in the Episcopal Church over the past few decades.

What is Spiritual Direction?

Words like *spiritual* and *direction* carry all sorts of open and hidden meanings that may not be true to what happens in practice. I see spiritual direction as a relationship within which one Christian accompanies someone else along the journey of faith towards maturity as a follower of Jesus Christ. It takes place in conversations that cover all aspects of life. It is privileged and confidential; its aim is to be as honest and open as possible. There is a clear recognition that God is important and present as a third party in the relationship, which unfolds against a background of prayer. In the Anglican tradition spiritual direction sometimes takes place in the context of sacramental confession and absolution, but probably less now than in the past.

Difficulties can also arise over the concept of *director* and *direction*. In the way we normally use them, the words carry a sense of authority, even authoritarianism. A director directs, is in charge. Directives are orders; you are supposed to comply with them, to obey. Obedience to a director has been seen by some people as an essential part of the relationship. But that kind of authoritarianism is foreign to many who are involved in spiritual direction today. What is essential is that the person seeking direction is fully respected as an independent human being. The director may discern, advise, and guide, but the other is free to decide.

Even the word *spiritual* may cause some problems. For most people it implies something to do with the soul, with prayer, with spirituality, itself an interesting word. Its use as a handy technical term is comparatively modern. Nowadays it is used to mean a person's inner life, a life of prayer.

It is also used with an adjective to describe a particular approach to prayer, like Franciscan or Ignatian or Anglican spirituality. It goes without saying that these matters are a proper, central concern within spiritual direction, but only as one aspect of our discipleship and service of Jesus Christ as whole persons. Every aspect of life is open to review. Prayer, work, family life, interests, leisure activities, relationships, fantasies and fears, hopes and disappointments are all the subject matter of spiritual direction. One of the gifts that the Ignatian revival has brought is the renewed emphasis that God can use anything and everything for people's growth in holiness and faithfulness.

So I have to accept that, as with so many technical terms, spiritual direction is not without its limitations and confusions. There are alternatives. John Wesley and the early Methodists talked of "spiritual guidance," while Reginald Somerset Ward and his successors have used "spiritual counsel," drawing on the prayer book phrase "ghostly counsel and advice." In 1974 Kenneth Leech's fine and influential book popularized the idea of "soul friend." But "spiritual direction" is the title that most people seem to recognize and is the one I intend to use.

There is difficulty too over what name to give the person who goes to someone else for spiritual direction. I have a personal reluctance to talk about a "directee": it is a word often used by British and American Roman Catholics and sometimes by Anglicans, but to me it feels foreign and a bit impersonal, with overtones of passivity. "Client" is also used frequently; it has advantages in the way it indicates the independence and authority of the individual. However, it also has strong overtones from the different disciplines of social work and psychotherapy. The nineteenth- and early twentieth-century directors spoke simply of "souls," but today this sounds rather too religious. Simply to say a "friend" is, I would hope, true, but perhaps it is also rather vague.

Perhaps the only clear way to describe the client is to use verbs. But which verb? Again there are overtones. Does one "consult" the director? "Go to" the director? "Use" the director? Is one "with" a director? Or "under"? All these alternatives are commonly used and each gives a different color to the relationship.

Even in this short space it is becoming clear that there is a wide range of what can be called spiritual direction. This is not surprising. A one-to-one relationship between two individuals, with God as the third party, gives room for infinite variety.

The experience of pastors suggests that we are living at a time when more and more people are looking for some kind of guidance. They value an opportunity for space and confidentiality to explore deep questions about the meaning and purpose of their life. This is true both within the church and in society at large. Spiritual direction is a ministry that the church has available to offer to these searchers. Certainly one of my aims in writing this book has been to give people who offer spiritual direction or those who are in training for it some idea of their Anglican inheritance. But another is to assure inquirers that help is available, and to encourage clergy and lay people within the church to make use of this ministry.

The Context of Spiritual Direction

When we take a look at the society in which we live, we have some mental picture of the past against which we compare today's world. I suspect that for many Christians it is a rather idealized image of security and strong faith in a previous age from which we have fallen away. The danger is that we so easily undervalue the positive strengths of contemporary life and attitudes.

In today's world religion is a matter of free choice. Whether or not our image of what happened in the past is true, we have to recognize that faith is no longer automatically handed on through family links, cultural heritage, or national identity. Like many other choices in life, faith is a matter of personal assent. The attitude that marks people in our society is not so much one of atheism or indifference as one of a perplexed uncertainty. Religious questions are not absent from people's minds; they just do not occupy an important place.

The past thirty years have witnessed a steady decrease in the number of churchgoers among westerners. Many but by no means all people who still do go to church show a more open relationship to their religion than before, with a greater desire for autonomy and more tolerance of different sorts of behaviors and attitudes. In many places people are beginning to recognize that the church is open to criticism from its own gospel. This recognition is, however, balanced by an opposing tendency that results in many new forms of fundamentalism.

Today we see an increased respect for personal responsibility, which has always been one of Anglicanism's basic tenets. People are often willing to consider what Christianity means without necessarily wanting to become a practicing member of any church. Faith is regarded as an aid in a personal search for a purpose and for a better quality of life. The Christian tradition is seen as a source of meaning from which one can draw freely, while at the same time preserving one's freedom and critical distance.

At its best, today's culture allows people to determine their own path in their search for meaning, free from any sort of coercion and indoctrination. Our secular and pluralistic society is faced with a superabundance of information and a wide variety of opinions, all constantly changing and often contradicting each other. It is deeply suspicious of bigotry. Any search for truth has to involve dialogue. Many, but by no means all, distrust any kind of proselytism. Faced by this kind of society, the church has two choices. It can be in the business of providing clear-cut, exclusive formulae for people to accept, which is the way many of the more conservative churches approach evangelism and Christian nurture. Or it can offer to accompany men and women as they are on their individual quest for meaning in life, in their search for truth and in their openness to a faith that contains both of these. The key values of this second and essentially non-violent attitude are open communication against a background of religious freedom; a willingness to adapt to people's different religious experiences and questions; and a profound willingness to stand where they stand and to respect their individuality. All these are qualities that I should look for in spiritual direction at its best.

The Anglican Tradition

I write as an Anglican raised in and belonging to the tradition and inheritance of the Church of England, and it is largely within that tradition that I am looking for particular insights into spiritual direction. There are many other Anglican streams, but the main thrust of this book is the Church of England and the Episcopal Church in America. However, no tradition of spiritual direction stands alone. The Church of England's inheritance in this area, as in so many others, draws on a number of sources beyond its own limits. There are deep currents of influence from eastern and western Christianity both before and after the Reformation. There is the inheritance from the faith of England in the Middle Ages. There are the insights that came through the upheaval of the Reformation on the Continent and in Britain. There is the life of the great Roman Catholic religious movements and the rediscovery of the relevance of Ignatian spirituality for today. There is a mass of new academic and practical work. All these have a bearing on the contemporary Anglican scene.

What interests me is to trace some lines that mark a specifically Anglican approach to spiritual direction and to note how people in our church show a particular attitude in the way they select and marry elements from this wide range of sources. To do this I shall need to look at some of the leading figures from our distant and recent past. Over the centuries there has been much variety in the value given to spiritual direction and to its effectiveness. There have been times when it was a recognized part of the pastoral ministry of our church, times when it suffered general neglect, and times when it was viewed with intense suspicion. I doubt whether there has ever been a time when Anglicans used the idea as freely as they do nowadays, though I believe we can claim that in practicing and making use of this ministry we are being utterly true to our roots.

Among my reasons for writing this book is the fact that the subject is important to me personally. Since I was in my early twenties I have had someone to whom I have gone for spiritual counsel. I know the value that it has been to me in my journey as a Christian and it is an increasingly large part of my ministry to be available to people who want to use me as a director. Both the receiving and the giving of spiritual direction are signs of God's grace and it is right that we should celebrate them. My second reason is more a matter of loyalty. In the surge of interest, writing, and training in the subject over the past fifteen years, a major influence has been the contemporary understanding of St. Ignatius of Loyola and his work. But Ignatius is not everything! I have been struck by the number of people who have complained, "This Ignatian revival is not the only approach! There *is* an Anglican tradition, too." True, I have thought, but what is it? This book is my attempt to answer that question.

Any tradition in the realm of spirituality and of spiritual direction draws on a wide range of insights and sources. Borrowings and adaptations from many different approaches and teachings within the wide-ranging Christian inheritance have helped to form our distinctive attitudes and approaches to this ministry. My loyalty to my own church pushes me to try to outline what has distinguished our way and marks it out as something special to thank God for. This is not to claim any exclusivity for the Anglican way, nor to say it is better than any other. It is simply to try to present it as one branch in the tree whose roots reach out to the one great River.

The third reason is also personal. A generation has passed since the death in 1962 of Reginald Somerset Ward. From about 1912 until he died, Ward served as a spiritual director to an enormous number of men and women. His vision and the counsel he gave shaped the lives not only of the people who came to him but also of those for whom they in turn cared. Of its nature this was a hidden ministry, intentionally so. For some years towards the end of his life I went to him as my director and for a long time after his death I was nurtured within the tradition that he began. So I write with a strong sense of *in piam memoriam*. His gifts under God feature large in any study of spiritual direction in the Anglican tradition.

Finally, as someone who believes strongly in the value of spiritual direction, I want to affirm those people who in whatever way give time to walk with others on their pilgrimage, whether in a formal organized way or simply as friends together. I have in mind both clergy and lay people who are already exercising this ministry, as well as those who are in different ways preparing to undertake it. I hope that this presentation of the inheritance into which they are entering will give them an assurance of its value and a sense that they have a crowd of companions with them on the road.

I also want to invite those who are trying to make sense of life, to find some sort of pattern in things, to realize that there is a resource in the church for them. Anyone who has worked in spiritual direction for some time knows very well that although part of their time is spent with committed Christians, more often than not with church members, there are other people who come to them from outside the boundaries of church. The openness of spiritual direction means that it offers a companionship without preconditions to people who take life seriously and want to deepen their awareness of the things that really matter.

As you read through the chapters I hope you will get the same strong impression I did in my research: that the Anglican tradition of spiritual direction, though it may not always have been known by that name, is one of openness to people, respect, and a genuine, loving desire for their good. Humane is a word that springs to mind to describe this tradition. The language it employs is one of healing and of growth rather than the language of the law court—judgment, condemnation, and punishment. Few of the people we will look at could be called vague or soft-hearted, but the pastoral roots of the Anglican tradition of spiritual direction mean that its practitioners are counselors, confessors, and physicians of the soul, not judges. There is warmth and a lightness of touch.

Allied with this warmth is the classic Anglican sense of moderation. The Anglican sensibility does not favor extremes; much of its counsel advises the common sense way. It endorses real religion but draws away from excessive religiosity. Its prayers may be deep, but they are simple, unfussy. Instead of over-pious scruples it values straightforward advice about everyday living. The Anglican way of spiritual direction has usually been local, low key, and practical.

It may sound contradictory, but I suspect that many of the people we shall survey would have shrunk from the label of "spiritual director." It is only fairly recently that the title has become respectable in the Anglican church; Edward Pusey, a wise and holy giver of spiritual counsel in the nineteenth century, refused to use it. I wonder whether this is because the Anglican tradition of authority resting in the Bible, church tradition, and human, God-given reason has given us a very strong respect for individual freedom and the right to make one's own decisions.

Also very much in the Anglican ethos is the wide variety of styles and approaches to spiritual direction. Clearly, there is no one way to do it. Technical skills are less respected than a closeness to God and a generosity of spirit. There is even a broad diversity in understanding what is actually meant by spiritual direction, all the way from two Christian friends walking together to the professional practice of a qualified person. The latter, however, is likely to be more acceptable in America than on the other side of the Atlantic; in Britain greater emphasis is placed on the director as a gifted amateur. Similarly, in the United States there is much greater overlap with counseling and psychotherapy.

Researching this book has meant meeting people who are active in this ministry and reading a range of different books by writers past and present. It has left me—and I hope it will leave you—with the heartening sense that in Anglicanism we can find a living and valid expression of Christian pastoring that is both true to our heritage and at the same time open to dialogue and exchange with what is best in other Christian traditions. I look forward to our growing in maturity, giving full value to our God-given diversity and open to the changes that growth in Christ brings.

Chapter 2

The English Pastoral Tradition

The model of the pastoral ministry of parish priests lies at the heart of Anglican spiritual direction. Phrases from the bishop's exhortation in the Ordering of Priests from the first *Book of Common Prayer* echo through instructions to the clergy and the life stories of the best of them over four centuries. Written in the reign of Edward VI, the words owe much to the influence of Martin Bucer, the German Reformation leader, who in 1549 came to England and was made Regius Professor of Divinity at Cambridge.

> Have in remembrance into how high a Dignity, and to how weighty an Office and Charge ye are called: that is to say, to be the Messengers, the Watchmen, the Pastors and the Stewards of the Lord; to teach, and to premonish, to feed and provide for the Lord's family; to seek for Christ's sheep, that are dispersed abroad and for his children in the midst of this naughty world, that they may be saved through Christ for ever.

> …See that you never cease your labour, your care and diligence, until you have done all that lieth in you, according to your bounden duty, to bring all such as are or shall be committed to your charge, unto that agreement in the faith and knowledge of God, and to that

ripeness and perfectness of age in Christ, that there be no place left among you, either for error in religion, or for viciousness in life.

The image that recurs through the centuries is that of priest as shepherd, exercising a personal ministry both in church and in people's homes. The ordained person is expected to be available to help people in trouble and go round the parish visiting. Because it is often so domestic, it is a hidden ministry that shuns publicity. Availability, willingness to be asked for counsel, and a loving openness to parishioners are all aspects of spiritual direction, though probably very few of those who ministered in this way would have accepted that label.

At the Reformation, the Church of England retained the geographical parish system and continued its living tradition of the parish priest. Since the sixteenth century the parson has had the cure of souls in the parish as the minister of Word and Sacrament. Even today people who are ordained in England are required to have a "title," a place within which they are to exercise their ministry. Ordination essentially implies a caring for and a responsibility to the people who live in a parish.

There are two aspects to what "pastoral" means. One is the model of the shepherd tending the hurt lamb, the Victorian Sunday school Jesus carrying home the lost sheep. Pastoring is thought of as care for the sick, for people with problems or special needs. It is about making things better, putting things right. There is also the broader understanding of enabling growth, development, and maturity. Obviously, these two understandings can overlap. If the pastor is concerned for personal growth, he or she has to be aware of and work with the problems in life that hinder that growth. Similarly, most pastors of people who are hurt or

sick have in mind their potential for maturity. Both these
sorts of pastor are to be found in the Anglican tradition of
spiritual direction, but I suggest that some of the best practice occurs when the director is primarily concerned for the
total overall growth of the person into the pattern of
Christ. Working with people's problems is a part of that. As
Reginald Somerset Ward wrote in his *Guide for Spiritual Directors*, published in 1957:

> The physician of souls has two equally important tasks,
> the first of which is to discover and to treat the spiritual
> hindrances to the health of the soul, and the second to
> develop and train the strengthening and quickening en-
> ergies in the life of the soul.[1]

Spirituality and spiritual direction are closely linked, but
they are not the same thing. Spirituality describes how
people pray, their deepest beliefs about God and about their
own nature. It is about their religious life or their spiritual
life, spilling over into the way they live and the spiritual
characteristics that mark their life. It can also be used more
broadly to refer to different methods of prayer or traditions
of prayer.

Spiritual direction is conversation about spiritual things
with someone who has made it their business to acquire
some knowledge and skill in the ways of prayer. To accompany people on their journey of faith, to help them grow
into the fullness of what God has it for them to become, is
to be concerned with every aspect of being. At the very
heart of that being is their openness to God and their response to God's invitation. Evelyn Underhill described
healthy detachment as "love without claimfulness," a de-
liberate listening for and seeking after God's interests in the
other's life, not my own interests or even the other person's.

Spiritual direction is about more than simply helping others with their prayers. It is to walk and work with people as they relate their faith with the practicalities of living the life that lies before them day by day. It is concerned with helping them to relate their faith in the context of the society and the relationships in which they live.

The only evidence we have of how people in the past understood spiritual direction is found in memoirs and biographies, in manuals of instruction or in the letters they wrote to people seeking their advice. It is not easy to imagine the actual conversations or to get a first-hand impression of the attitudes and relationships that are the heart of direction. It is also difficult to put oneself back in time into a society very different from today's and to enter with sympathy into a world of attitudes, expectations, and pressures foreign to our own. We need, therefore, to avoid the danger of superimposing our culture, our experiences and prejudices on the stories of people from the past. We have to listen as openly as we can to the evidence of earlier writers without picking and choosing the ideas that seem appropriate for today and discarding others that jar us or seem unpalatable.

"The Cloud of Unknowing" and Julian of Norwich

In the pages that follow I draw on the writings of a number of people who in their lives and ministries demonstrated the Anglican "middle way" and showed that care for their parishioners' growth in Christ-likeness that is the hallmark of spiritual direction. The tradition they represent goes back a long way, reaching through the English mystics of the Middle Ages, through those who influenced them, like Bernard of Clairvaux and the great St. Augustine of Hippo, to the desert fathers and mothers of the early church. Finally, the roots reach deep into Scripture itself.

Among the English spiritual writers of the Middle Ages there are two in particular from the fourteenth century who have come to the fore in the twentieth and played a part in shaping contemporary spirituality. The name of one we do not know; he is simply known as the author of *The Cloud of Unknowing*. The other we call Dame Julian of Norwich, though it is likely that the name "Julian" comes from the dedication of the church in Norwich where she lived as an anchoress and may well not be her own name. Both *The Cloud* and Julian's *Revelations of Divine Love* were written to help Christians grow in their openness to God and discipleship and reflect a particular style of spiritual direction.

The Cloud of Unknowing is one of the devotional classics of the English church. It is written as a series of instructions in contemplation given by an older man to a younger novice in that way of praying. All that we know about the author has to be gleaned from the text itself. Its editor, Clifton Wolters, writes in his introduction that

> every reader will form his own opinion of the author. He was a man convinced of the necessity for God to be at the centre of all life; he had a well stored and scholarly mind, with a flair for expressing complexities simply; there was more than a streak of the poet in him, and at the same time a saving sense of humour and proportion. Probably most people would feel they would like to know him, and some at least might wish they could have his guidance today.
>
> We may guess that he was a country parson, perhaps in the East Midlands, with more than a nodding acquaintance of the religious life and a largish circle of souls under his direction.[2]

This unknown author designed *A Book on Contemplation called The Cloud of Unknowing in which a soul is united with God* to offer guidance for someone entering on the way of contemplative prayer. One gets the strong feeling that what is written there is the fruit of many interviews and meetings with people who had come to the writer for just that sort of advice.

Julian's *Revelations* spring from her own vivid spiritual experiences during a life-threatening illness. The book is a record of the reflections she made on them throughout her long life. In spite of their deeply personal nature, they are written to help "the even Christians," the ordinary men and women trying to follow their Lord. Margery Kempe, a contemporary from Kings Lynn, has left an account of her visit to Julian to ask for advice about her own visions; presumably she was one of many lay men and women who went to Julian in her cell by the church to consult her. Julian herself was quite clear that the gifts she had been given were meant to be shared:

> Everything that I say about myself I mean to apply to all my fellow Christians, for I am taught that this is what our Lord intends in this spiritual revelation. But God forbid that you should say or assume that I am a teacher, for that is not and never was my intention; for I am a woman, ignorant, weak and frail. But I know very well that what I am saying I have received by the revelation of him who is the sovereign teacher.[3]

The result is both a homely theological treatise on the love God shows in creation and through the death of Jesus on the cross, and also a deeply committed work of personal prayer and devotion.

The Spirituality of the Prayer Book

At its very simplest the spirituality of Anglicanism could be expressed in just two principles: "Go to church and try to live a good life." It concerns itself with our duty towards God and towards our neighbor, based on the Ten Commandments. In that summary of Christian instruction there is something essentially Anglican. Nothing is exaggerated about it: moderation is one of the keys to Anglicanism and expresses its search for a middle way between extremes, a balance that is aided by its constant appeal to Scripture, history, reason, and experience. This attitude underlies the characteristically Anglican regard for common sense solutions, simplicity, and practicality. Its spirituality is marked by tolerance, has its roots firmly in the Bible, is expressed in a particular liturgy, and is grounded in everyday life. The real test lies in how Anglicans live out what they say they believe.

The Book of Common Prayer, first produced in 1549, has been a constant influence on Anglican spirituality, both in England and America. In the middle of the twentieth century the widespread movement for liturgical renewal encouraged many churches to rewrite their services, including the 1662 prayer book of the Church of England and the American prayer book of 1928. The general use of the *Alternative Service Book* of 1980, the American *Book of Common Prayer* of 1979, and other modern liturgies throughout the churches of the Anglican Communion has meant that for the first time since the Reformation Anglicans no longer instinctively react to familiar words and phrases from the prayer book, though many of the principles that underlay it still hold good for them.

Since churchgoing is an important aspect of Anglican spirituality, it is not surprising that prayer book worship in the parish church has had a deep and continuing influence.

In a persuasive article Gordon Mursell claims that the *Book of Common Prayer* "is in fact and was intended to be as much a manual of spiritual guidance as a directory of public services.... Behind this guidance lay a pattern of spirituality concerned to integrate the secular and the sacred, in both their corporate and personal dimensions."[4]

Simplicity and directness mark the *Book of Common Prayer*. Its language is designed to be understood by the people of its day and its concerns are immediate to their lives. This balance of prayer and everyday life is reflected in a balance between faith and theology on the one hand and worship and spirituality on the other. As the seventeenth-century bishop Jeremy Taylor wrote, "Public forms of prayer are great advantages to convey an article of faith into the most secret retirements of the spirit, and to establish it with a most firm persuasion and endear it to us with the greatest affection." Echoing this sentiment is Bishop Beveridge's 1681 sermon on the prayer book: that it contained everything Christians ought to believe, everything they ought to do, and everything for which they ought to ask or pray.

In the *Book of Common Prayer* there are prayers to mark both regular ordinary events and occasions of special need in personal life or in national emergency. After childbirth, in storms at sea, or during times of war you find that the realities of the situation are part of the prayers offered. The core of the human side of prayer is life as it is lived, which includes facing up to the fact of death. The compilers clearly hoped that lay people would take part in the daily offices of morning and evening prayer, and the church bell was ordered to be rung before the service to remind them. At the beginning of the daily office in the English prayer book the invitation to confession outlines the purpose of daily common prayer, which is "to render thanks for the great benefits that we have received at [God's] hands, to set forth his most worthy praise, and to hear his most holy Word, and to ask those things that are requisite and necessary as well for the body as the soul."

The claim that the prayer book has a place in the story of Anglican spiritual direction is also supported by the links between the Anglican ethos and the Benedictine monastic tradition. Benedictine spirituality has had a strong influence on the prayer book, according to the Benedictine Bede Mudge:

> The example and influence of the Benedictine monastery, with its rhythm of divine office and Eucharist, the tradition of learning and "lectio divina," and the family relationship among Abbot and community were determinative for much of English life, and for the pattern of English devotion. This devotional pattern persevered through the spiritual and theological upheavals of the Reformation. The Book of Common Prayer...the primary spiritual source-book for Anglicans...continued the basic monastic pattern of the Eucharist and the divine office as the principal public forms of worship and Anglicanism has been unique in this respect.[5]

The Caroline Divines

The poet and priest George Herbert stands out among early writers about parish ministry. He had spent some years at the court of James I before leaving to become the rector of Bemerton, a small village near Salisbury. From his experience there he wrote *The Country Parson*, a book that vividly illustrates the way in which the good pastor of his day might be expected to fulfill his ministry in its many different aspects. For instance, he writes about "the parson as father":

> The Country Parson is not only a Father to his flock, but
> also professeth himself thoroughly of the opinion, car-
> rying it about with him as fully as if he had begot his
> whole parish. For by this means, when any sins, he
> hateth him not as an Officer, but pities him as a Father.[6]

Here, "officer" means "policeman" and the contrast is as
vivid today as it was then. Discussing the work of the priest
among people in special need, Herbert writes about "the
parson comforting":

> In visiting the sick, or otherwise afflicted, he followeth
> the Church's counsel, namely, in persuading them to
> particular confession, labouring to make them under-
> stand the great good use of this ancient ordinance and
> how necessary it is in some cases.

Although Herbert's description of "the parson in journey"
may describe a social scene long past, the attitudes he recom-
mends are true for any age. He envisages his country parson
staying in a house on his journey and noting "failures in ap-
parel, diet or behaviour, or in piety":

> As he finds any defect in these, he first considers with
> himself what kind of remedy fits the temper of the
> house best and then he faithfully and boldly applieth it;
> yet seasonably and discreetly, by taking aside the Lord
> or Lady or master and mistress of the house and show-
> ing them clearly that they respect them most who wish
> them best and that not a desire to meddle with others'
> affairs but the earnestness to do all the good he can
> moves him to say thus and thus.

The Caroline divines also include several recognized
spiritual theologians within the tradition of the Church of
England, among them Lancelot Andrewes. Along with

Richard Hooker he was among those responsible for a reformed Anglican theology. A remarkable scholar, he became
successively Bishop of Ely, Chichester, and Winchester. From
the point of view of spiritual direction we owe him a debt for
his *Preces Privatae*, a collection of prayers in Greek and Latin
for his own use. They draw heavily on texts from Scripture
and were very influential in the development of later spirituality. Richard Hooker was the leading theologian and
apologist of the settlement under Elizabeth I, whose *Of the
Laws of Ecclesiastical Polity* is one of the foundational docu-
ments of the reformed church.

Joseph Hall was a moderate Puritan who became bishop
first of Exeter and then of Norwich. His *Meditations* have
been described as a Protestant alternative for *The Spiritual
Exercises* of St. Ignatius, with their clear guidance for the
person who prays:

> Those that meditate by snatches and uncertain fits,
> when only all other employments forsake them, or
> when good motions are forced upon them by necessity,
> let them never hope to reach to any perfection. Set thine
> hours, and keep them; and yield not to an easy distrac-
> tion. There is no hardness in this practice, but in the be-
> ginning; use shall give it, not ease only, but delight.[7]

Thomas Ken served as a chaplain in the royal household
and was Bishop of Bath and Wells until, with the deposition
of James II, he was one of the "Non-Jurors" who refused to
take the oath of obedience to the new King William III. He
wrote the morning and evening hymns "Awake, my soul,
and with the sun" and "All praise to thee, my God, this
night." Ken's treatise entitled *Practice of Divine Love; being
an Exposition on the Church Catechism* contains this prayer:

Thou, O heavenly Guide of our devotion and our love, by teaching us to pray hast shewed us that Prayer is our Treasury where all our strength and weapons are stored, the only great preservative, and the very vital heat of divine love. Give me grace to call on thee at all times by diligent prayer. Lord, I know my devotion has daily interruptions, and I cannot always be actually praying. All I can do is to beg of thy love to keep my heart always in an habitual disposition to devotion, and in mindfulness of thy divine presence. As thy infinite love is ever-streaming in blessings on me, O let my soul be ever breathing love to thee.[8]

His treatment of the Ten Commandments continues this theme of the importance of daily prayer. Ken offers prayers that follow from the various sections and simple examples for daily prayer in the morning and the evening, including:

As soon as ever you awake, offer up your first thoughts and words to God saying, "Glory be to the Father, and to the Son, and to the Holy Ghost, three persons and one God, blessed for evermore: all love, all praise be to thee."

A selection of short prayers for various occasions includes suggestions for us "at going out or coming in," "in the shop or market," "after a sin committed," "after any blessing or deliverance," and "after having done any good." Elsewhere Ken gives his vision of the ideal priest, which is as good a description of a spiritual director as I can find:

Give me a priest, a light upon a hill,
Whose rays his whole circumference fill,
In God's own word and Sacred Learning versed,
Deep in the study of the heart immersed,

Who in such souls can the disease descry,
And wisely fair restoratives supply.

The Caroline divines reveal a very practical side to Anglican spirituality. Certainly it is about a relationship with God, but there is never any doubt that this relationship has to be lived out in ordinary life. The mark of a Christian is how you behave with other people. The Church of England at the Reformation retained confession and absolution as part of the ministry of the priest. Within this ministry there was the opportunity not merely for the assurance of forgiveness but also for spiritual and practical counsel. The passage in the prayer book commending this is found in one of the exhortations before Holy Communion:

> Because it is requisite that no man should come to Holy Communion, but with a full trust in God's mercy, and with a quiet conscience; therefore if there be any of you, who cannot quiet his own conscience, but require further counsel and comfort, then let him come to me, or to some other discreet and learned Minister of God's Word and open his grief, that by the Ministry of God's holy Word he may receive the benefit of absolution, to the quieting of his conscience, and avoiding of all scruple and doubtfulness.

Anglican continuity is well shown in the way in which one of the most recent liturgies of *A New Zealand Prayer Book* similarly describes the rite of reconciliation:

> Scripture makes it clear that whenever a sinner turns to God in penitence, forgiveness follows. In addition, to reassure the conscience of those who continue to remain troubled, and to provide a discipline that many find beneficial, the Church offers this ministry of reconciliation.

In it the priest, on behalf of the Christian community, listens to the penitent's confession of sins and declares God's forgiveness.

The penitent is thus enabled to express the source of guilt, and the priest offers counsel and the assurance of reconciliation.[9]

A commentary on the original invitation to confession is found in a book written in the middle of the seventeenth century, *The Whole Duty of Man,* which is of uncertain authorship. It is designed to be read a section a week as part of Sunday devotions. On the third Sunday we find a careful passage that expands the note on private confession in the prayer book exhortation:

If any person upon a serious view of himself cannot satisfy his own soul of his sincerity, and so doubts whether he may come to the sacrament, he do not rest wholly on his own judgement in the case. For if he be a truly humbled soul, it is likely he may judge too hardly of himself; if he be not, it is odds, but if he be left to the satisfying of his own doubts, he will quickly bring himself to pass too favourable a sentence.

I would exhort him not to trust to his own judgement, but to make known his case to some discreet and godly Minister, and rather be guided by his, who will probably (if the case be duly and without any disguise discovered to him) be better able to judge of him than he himself. This is the counsel the Church gives in the Exhortation before Communion.

The truth is, we are generally so apt to favour ourselves, that it might be very useful for the most, especially for the most ignorant sort, sometimes to advise with a spiritual guide, to enable them to pass right judgements on themselves; and not only so, but to receive directions on how to subdue and mortify those sins they are most inclined to, which is a matter of so much difficulty, that we have no reason to despise any means that may help us in it.[10]

Jeremy Taylor's life spanned the reign of Charles I, the Civil War, the period of the Commonwealth, and the restoration of the monarchy under Charles II. At one time a chaplain to the king and later a chaplain in the royalist army, Taylor was briefly imprisoned under Oliver Cromwell and later withdrew to a kind of internal exile in Wales. In 1660 he was made Bishop of Down and Connor. He is perhaps best known for his *Holy Living and Holy Dying.* In the dedication to that work, written at the close of the Commonwealth, he speaks of the upheavals that have affected the nation and church, not least the scattering of the parish clergy and others like himself:

> I thought I had reasons enough inviting me to draw into one body those advices which the several necessities of many men must use at some time or other, and many of them daily; that by a collection of holy precepts they might less feel the want of personal and attending guides, and that the rules for the conduct of souls might be committed to a book which they might always have; since they could not always have a prophet at their needs, nor be suffered to go up to the house of the Lord to inquire of the appointed oracles.[11]

This "want of personal and attending guides" that was the result of the troubles in church and state indicates that Taylor himself, and presumably many Anglican pastors like him, believed that it was right for people to look to a personal guide for help in spiritual and moral matters. It was in a charge to the clergy of his diocese of Down and Connor in 1661 that he encouraged his clergy "to exhort their people to a frequent confession of their sins, and a declaration of the state of their souls; to a conversation with their minister in spiritual things; to an enquiry concerning all parts of their duty."

Holy Living and *Holy Dying* are each made up of essays on aspects of the Christian life and rules for living. Among his "general instruments and means serving to a holy life," Taylor offers "care of our time, purity of intention, and practice of the presence of God." He suggests themes for meditation and many prayers, some general and some for specific occasions. It does not take much imagination to see behind the written word the highly intelligent and compassionate man who wrote them, and to sense how he would have conversed with individuals on topics vital for the life of the Christian.

Among the other great figures of this age to whom Anglicans look back with gratitude for their spiritual and intellectual gifts are John Donne, Dean of St. Paul's and one of the great preachers and poets of his age, Archbishop William Laud, and Nicholas Ferrar. Ferrar founded the Little Gidding community, which was a group of families, about forty people in all, living together under a simple rule of corporate prayer and service.

William Law was in the second generation of the Non-Jurors; he found himself unable to swear the oath of obedience at the accession of George I. He left his Cambridge fellowship for a life in private chaplaincy and in the establishment of a simple religious household devoted to works of charity and education. He was a gifted writer and used his skill in two markedly different sorts of Christian books. *A Serious Call to a Devout and Holy Life* opens with the sentence, "Devotion is neither private nor public prayer; but prayers, whether private or public, are particular parts or instances of devotion. Devotion signifies a life given, or devoted to, God." Law goes on to develop this insight that the spiritual life and the practical are two aspects of the same commitment:

> As sure, therefore, as there is any wisdom in praying for the Spirit of God, so sure is it, that we are to make that Spirit the rule of all our actions; as sure as it is our duty to look wholly unto God in our prayers, so sure is it that it is our duty to live wholly unto God in our lives. But we can no more be said to live unto God, unless we live unto Him in all the ordinary actions of our life, unless he be the rule and measure of all our ways, than we can be said to pray unto God, unless our prayers look wholly unto Him.

For much of the book Law makes use of character sketches and stories taken from the well-to-do milieu of the audience for which he was writing, to illustrate various ways of living out the Christian life and the temptations that lie in the path of different kinds of people. It is not easy to identify with many of the lives Law describes because the underlying attitudes are so foreign to the way we think today. But his remarks about Callidus, the over-busy businessman, point to someone instantly recognizable:

> Callidus has traded above thirty years in the greatest city of the kingdom; he has been so many years constantly increasing his trade and his fortune. Every hour of his day is with him an hour of business; and though he eats and drinks very heartily, yet every meal seems to be in a hurry, and he would say grace if he had time. Callidus ends every day at the tavern, but has not lei-

sure to be there till nine o'clock. He is always forced to drink a good hearty glass, to drive thoughts of business out of his head, and make his spirits drowsy enough for sleep. He does business all the time he is rising, and has settled several matters before he can get to his counting room. His prayers are a short ejaculation or two, which he never misses in stormy, tempestuous weather, because he has always something or other at sea. Callidus will tell you, with great pleasure, that he has been in this hurry for so many years, and that it must have killed him long ago, but that it has been a rule with him to get out of the town every Saturday, and make the Sunday a day of quiet and good refreshment in the country.

If thoughts of religion happen at any time to steal into his head, Callidus contents himself with thinking, that he never was a friend to heretics and infidels, that he has always been civil to the minister of his parish and very often given something to charity schools.[12]

I recognize in William Law a man who could listen with accuracy and who could respond with discernment. He had a lively interest in people and everything about them. Certainly his *Serious Call* has been a classic of Anglican spiritual and practical advice for three centuries.

In the later part of his life Law's spirituality and writing changed as a result of his reading the works of Jacob Boehme, the seventeenth-century German Lutheran mystical author. As Evelyn Underhill wrote:

Through the interpretations of his great disciple, William Law, [Boehme's] teachings brought their renewing touch to English institutionalism at one of the most deadly moments in its career. Law's few mystical writings were produced in the later part of his life; for Boehme's influence reached him in middle age. We cannot doubt that he experienced that interior transformation that he passionately proclaims; and which turned the brilliant ecclesiastic into the gentle and saintly recluse and director of souls who wrote *The Spirit of Prayer, The Way to Divine Knowledge* and *The Spirit of Love.*[13]

In these later books Law's weighty emphasis on behavior is gone and has been replaced by a fervor for God himself, as in *The Spirit of Prayer:*

Nothing is so strong, so irresistible as divine love. It brought forth all the creation; it kindles all the life of heaven, it is the song of all the angels of God. It has redeemed all the world; it seeks for every sinner upon earth; it embraces all the enemies of God and from the beginning to the end of time the one work of providence is the one work of love.

Ask what God is? His name is love; he is the good, the perfection, the peace, the joy, the glory and blessing of every life. Ask what Christ is? He is the universal remedy broken forth in nature and creatures.

From what are almost caricatures of human behaviour in *A Serious Call,* Law turns inward to recognize the vital importance of the will. In *An Answer to Dr. Trapp,* he claims that

it is the state of our will that makes the state of our life; when we receive anything from God and do everything for God, everything does us the same good and helps us to the same degree of happiness.

When we thus live wholly unto God, God is wholly ours and we are happy in all that happiness of God. For in uniting with him in heart and will and spirit we are united to all that he is and has in himself.

In union with God, we realize that prayer

is not silence, or a simple petition, or a great variety of outward expressions that alters the nature of prayer, or makes it better, but only and solely the reality, steadiness and continuity of the desire; and therefore whether a man offers this desire to God in the silent longing of the heart, or in simple short petitions, or in a great variety of words is of no consequence. But if you would know what I would call a true and great gift of prayer, and what I most wish for myself, it is a good heart that stands continually inclined towards God.[14]

Eighteenth-Century Anglicanism

It is a commonly held view that the Church of England went through an arid period in the eighteenth century, at least as far as spiritual fervor is concerned. There are far fewer theologians and preachers of a spiritual depth that is comparable to that of the Caroline divines. Although he did not die until 1761, in a sense William Law's life and work can been seen as marking the close of that era of Anglicanism. He was an important influence on Anglicans who came after him, such as Samuel Johnson, the eighteenth-century lexigrapher, biographer, and man of letters. Johnson was also a man of committed religious belief and practice, and it was William Law's *Serious Call*, he claimed, that brought him to this commitment. He was a strong high churchman, sincere in his prayer and worship and very generous to those in need. His essay on friendship in *The Rambler* is worth reading for the light it sheds on the relationship of friendship and spiritual direction:

We are often by superficial accomplishments and accidental endearments, induced to love those whom we cannot esteem; we are sometimes, by great abilities and incontestable evidences of virtues, compelled to esteem those we whom cannot love. But friendship, compounded of esteem and love, derives from one its tenderness, and its permanence from the other; and therefore requires not only that its candidates should gain the judgement, but that they should attract the affections; that they should not only be firm in the day of distress, but gay in the hour of jollity; not only useful in exigencies, but pleasing in familiar life; their presence should give cheerfulness as well as courage, and dispel alike the gloom of fear and of melancholy.[15]

The eighteenth century gives us the picture of an established church thoroughly aligned with the society of the day and, if not exactly corrupt, certainly infected with worldly values. Throughout this period, however, the regular pastoral work of the clergy continued; worship was maintained and the Christian faith was preached and taught. Parson Woodeford's diaries recounting his life as a Norfolk incumbent may be famous for the description of gargantuan meals eaten in his own parsonage or out as a guest in the grander houses of the neighborhood, but they also record his faithful reading of Sunday prayers and his visiting of the people in his parish.

In sharp contrast to this picture of an "establishment" church is the ministry of John and Charles Wesley and that of their companions in early Methodism. In a later chapter I shall look in more detail at the evangelical revival; here my interest is in the ministry of spiritual guidance, which was an essential part of the Wesleyan revival. Even wealthy bankers like Ebenezer Blackwell needed a spiritual guide, as Wesley wrote to him:

> I am fully persuaded, if you had always one or two faithful friends near you who would speak the very truth from their heart and watch over you in love, you would swiftly advance.[16]

Much pastoral care took place within the context of the classes and bands of the converts and their leaders. It is clear, however, that men like the Wesleys and their ministerial colleagues, together with prominent women, exercised a personal ministry of guidance. The need for such companionship was ever present, as Wesley remarked in one letter:

> It is a blessed thing to have fellow travellers to New Jerusalem. If you cannot find any you must make them; for none can travel the road alone.

Wesley's correspondence with Ann Bolton, a leading woman in the movement, lasted for nearly thirty years. The ninety-three letters that remain show him to be an effective spiritual guide to a woman of developing faith who found her own calling in ministering both to groups and individuals, as well as being a spiritual guide. Their correspondence reveals Wesley's warm affection for those under his guidance. As one scholar notes, "Hundreds of expressions of uncommon affection punctuate Wesley's letters of guidance. One must believe that no model of spiritual guidance which does not emphasise love could be accurately called Wesleyan." In a letter written to Nancy Bolton during one of her frequent illnesses, he prescribes chewing bark, eating all the red currants she could, and remembering the love of God. An emphasis on reciprocal openness also recurs in these letters, as in this reply to Ebenezer Blackwell:

> You do well to warn me against "popularity, a thirst for power and applause,…against an affected humility, against sparing from myself to give to others from no other motives than ostentation." I am not conscious to myself that this is my case. However, the warning is always friendly, always seasonable, considering how deceitful my heart is and how many the enemies that surround me.

Here is a strong, positive note of encouragement as well as Wesley's belief that it was the duty of Christians to hold each other spiritually accountable as they journeyed towards the New Jerusalem, seen in this life as entire sanctification, or Christian perfection.

John Wesley himself lived and died a priest in the Church of England, so it is proper to include him in the Anglican story. However, it also has to be remembered that the Anglican church as a whole found itself unable to contain the renewal with which Methodism challenged it. Wesley's claim to view the whole world as his parish cut across traditional boundaries; the emotional warmth and direct challenge of his preaching produced opposition among the pillars of the established church. Certainly there were those who were greatly affected by this revival and yet stayed within Anglicanism, and we shall visit them later in the book.

Endnotes

1. Reginald Somerset Ward, *A Guide for Spiritual Directors* (London and Oxford: Mowbray, 1957), 45.

2. Clifton Wolters, ed., *The Cloud of Unknowing* (London: Penguin, 1961), 11.

3. *Julian of Norwich: Showings* (London: SPCK, 1978), 133.

4. Gordon Mursell, *The Way* (April 1991), 163.

5. Quoted in Robert Hale, *Canterbury and Rome: Sister Churches* (London: Darton, Longman &Todd, 1982), 91.

6. Quotations from George Herbert's *The Country Parson* are from the 1853 edition (Pickering, London).

7. Quoted in P. Handley, ed., *The English Spirit* (London: Darton, Longman &Todd, 1987), 81.

8. Quotations from Thomas Ken are from the 1838 edition of *Prose Works* (Rivington, London).

9. *A New Zealand Prayer Book* (Auckland: Collins, 1989), 750.

10. Quoted in Paul E. More and Frank L. Cross, *Anglicanism* (London: SPCK, 1951), 513.

11. Jeremy Taylor, *Holy Living and Holy Dying* (London: Bohn, 1850).

12. William Law, *A Serious Call to a Devout and Holy Life* (London: SPCK, 1978), 47; 48; 80.

13. Evelyn Underhill, *The Mystics of the Church* (London: James Clarke, 1925), 231.

14. Quoted in Robert Llewelyn and Edward Moss, eds., *Fire from a Flint: Daily Readings with William Law* (London: Darton, Longman & Todd, 1986), 2; 11; 39.

15. Quoted in David Hein's essay "Spiritual Counsel in the Anglican Tradition," *Anglican Theological Review* 77:204.

16. Quotations from the letters of John Wesley are from Wesley D. Tracy's essay "John Wesley, Spiritual Director," *Wesleyan Theological Journal* 23:149.

Chapter 3

The Catholic Revival

The Oxford Movement's revival of the catholic and sacramental tradition of the Church of England is of great
importance in the story of spiritual direction. Faced with
what they saw as a decline in the vigor of church life, Anglican clergy like John Keble and Edward Pusey worked to recover and promote the awareness of the Church of England
not simply as an appendage of the state but as God's holy
church. To recover this vision, they looked back both to the
Middle Ages and to the high points of seventeenth-century
theology and devotion. A sermon preached by John Keble
at Oxford in 1833, occasioned by the suppression of ten
bishoprics in Ireland and later entitled "National Apos-
tasy," is usually credited with being the start of the movement. The publication of *Tracts for the Times*, which John
Henry Newman also began in that year, provided a continuing focus and means of communication for the beliefs
of the movement.

The rediscovery of the catholic inheritance of the
Church of England brought a renewed emphasis on both
the eucharist and on the sacrament of confession and absolution. This is not the place to enter deeply into the stories
of conflict that marked the Victorian church—there were
certainly plenty of those—but to note that in their search
for the catholic gifts in the church the leaders of the Oxford
Movement looked both to the classic Anglican writers of

the Reformation and to the Continent, particularly to the French Roman Catholic theologians of the Counter Reformation. The introduction of their ideas and practices caused great upheaval in the Church of England at the time, though much of what they struggled for with regard to ritual has become normal practice for Anglicans.

John Keble

Born in the last decade of the eighteenth century, John Keble was a scholar, poet, and parish priest. As we have seen, his sermon in 1833 while a fellow of Oriel College was the flash point for the Oxford Movement, and he was deeply involved in *Tracts for the Times*. From his books of poems come several well-loved hymns, "New every morning is the love" and "Blest are the pure in heart" among them. More significantly for his contribution to spiritual direction, not long after his death a collection of Keble's *Letters of Spiritual Counsel and Guidance* was published. These letters came from different times in his life but show a remarkable consistency in style and attitudes. The editor of the volume, R. S. Wilson, took great pains to hide the identity of the people to whom Keble wrote, even to the extent of not giving a date to the majority of the letters, which range from 1817 to 1865. Many of them were written at some speed and give an impression of immediacy. As Wilson remarked in his introduction, the letters were brief and far from systematic because Keble supplemented them with personal meetings of spiritual direction.

Repeatedly Keble speaks of his own unworthiness to advise, as he writes to a young woman who had consulted him about her wish to join a sisterhood:

> How little do you know what sort of a person you are consulting, on so very sacred a matter! But let that pass;

worthy or unworthy, my office binds me to do my best for a Christian person who thinks I can help him; and it will indeed be a comfort, of which I am quite unworthy, if I am enabled to be of any use or consolation to you.[1]

His editor's comment on Keble's expressed reticence was clearly based not only on the letters but even more on his personal acquaintance with Keble:

It is quite possible that in this exceeding backwardness and self-distrust there may have been some admixture of timidity, or other natural imperfection; but it chiefly arose from that most rare humility and self-depreciation which had become so ingrained in all he did and said as to be part of his very self. You could hardly ask his opinion on a matter of any difficulty, on which his advice would not be given with this sort of hesitancy; so much so, as sometimes to leave persons uncertain what he really meant to counsel or direct, or whether he had made up his mind on the matter. But this conclusion would have been entirely mistaken. With him...expressions of uncertainty did not rightly convey doubt on his own part about the matter, so much as the habitual uprising thought, "Who was he, that he should advise anybody?"

This description of Keble's humility is reinforced by something Keble himself wrote to a close friend:

For myself, my inward history is a most shameful and miserable one, really quite different from what you and others imagine; so that I am quite sure, if you knew it, you would be startled at the thought of coming to such an adviser, so long and so late has the misery been; and it ought to be a bitter penance to me to be so consulted. But I believe that I have sinned before now, in drawing back on such occasions, and I hope never to do so again; use me therefore, dear friend, such as I am if I can be of any use to you at any time; but pray for me, *bona fide*, that I may be contrite, for that is what I really need.

Reading through his *Letters of Spiritual Counsel and Guidance*, I am struck by Keble's deep care for the people he is writing to and by the sense of sound balance that pervades his answers to their questions. Whether it is a matter of practical choices in life or of problems and challenges in the life of prayer, there are strong marks of his own spiritual experience, of his insight and openness to the other person's situation, and of his straightforward common sense. For instance, when someone consulted him about a young woman's religious scruples, Keble wrote in reply:

I am clearly of the opinion that the young lady should discontinue those observances which seem to fret and distract her so much.... Clearly this is a case of melancholy from bodily constitution, and the person should be recommended to avoid all vows and singularities of every kind as mere snares.

Keble then refers his correspondent to what the Anglican theologian Jeremy Taylor had to say in *Ductor Dubitantium:*

Let the scrupulous man avoid all excess in mortifications and corporal austerities because these are apt to trouble the body and consequently disorder the mind. Let the scrupulous man interest himself in as few questions of intricate dispute and minute disquisitions as he can. That religion is best, which is incorporated with the actions and common traverses of our life.

In a similar vein, Keble wrote to a man who was newly ordained to the priesthood about the danger of too strict a spiritual discipline:

Even in my narrow round of experience, I have seen so much that is really injurious to truth and piety arising from that view of the Christian life which I understand you incline to, that I am truly grieved whenever I hear of any of my friends taking it up. I do not mean that it is possible for a man to be too much in earnest about religion, or to give up too much of his time to it: on the contrary, he who takes the injunction "do all to the glory of God" in the most literal sense, appears to me to come nearest to the true sense of it.... Self denial seems to mean not going out of the world, but walking warily and uprightly in it.

Then, as he so often does, Keble invokes the authority of Scripture as he continues:

My impression has been formed a good deal, I believe, by the seventh chapter of the first epistle to the Corinthians, not from any direct precepts but from the general tenor and tone of its morality.

Writing to a woman friend about spiritual dryness, Keble suggests that it may have a physical cause:

One thing I *will* say, for I am most firmly persuaded of it, that a great part of your dullness and dryness about holy things, probably the whole, so far as it is accountable by human judgement, is a symptom of your illness: and I daresay you often feel the like distressing want of interest in other matters which you would fain take an interest in.

Do not be too severe, do not strain your inward eye by turning it too violently back upon itself: remember you are bound for others' sake, as well as your own, to be, if you can, and not only to seem, comfortable and cheerful.

Keble's correspondence on spiritual direction also contains a series of letters to a woman on her distress at the absence of conscious love and devotion in her prayers:

I am much confirmed in my opinion that your distress is in a great measure what may be called "morbid feeling" and that the way to deal with it is not so much by direct opposition as by refusing to attend to it, turning the mind another way. Pray against it beforehand, but do not brood over it when it comes. I have no doubt that if another person were to come to you with the same kind of trouble in heart, you would say to him, "If you had no kind of love for God, you would not be troubled at your want of love for Him."

Another letter is to an aged clergyman suffering spiritual depression. Particularly interesting is the fact that the letter is accompanied by a note from the person who sent it to Keble's editor in the first place. Describing the clergyman's final illness, he writes:

My relative was dying at an advanced age, though with unimpaired faculties; his body gradually wearing out without any pain or disease: but he was oppressed with a deep sense of his sinfulness, and fear that he had not been forgiven, and consequent absence of all comfort in prayer. One day in answer to a suggestion to consult some others, the words burst from him. "Oh that John Keble were here." I at once, though a stranger to Keble, wrote to him, describing as well as I could the state of mind. It drew from him the letter of which I enclose a copy. Some days after its receipt he looked up to me suddenly and said, "I am quite happy now," and in the same quiet happiness of faith he died.

Keble's response to the old man gives a clear and forceful reminder of God's love for all, and he suggests that it is through recognizing our own humility that we are able to cast all our care on God. He closes with these words:

> My dear Sir, excuse my running on in this way: sometimes the merest truism put in the homeliest way may help where a higher sort of teaching has failed or might fail. But I trust that you will have more and more of that inward comfort and teaching which makes the soul happily independent of human suggestions, however well meant.

Edward Bouverie Pusey

The second key figure of the Oxford Movement I want to look at is Edward Bouverie Pusey, who was born in 1800 and lived through most of the decade. He became the movement's acknowledged leader when John Henry Newman was received into the Roman Catholic Church; his followers were sometimes known as "Puseyites." In 1846 Pusey preached a ground-breaking sermon at Oxford called "The Entire Absolution of the Penitent," which marked the beginning of the recovery of the practice of formal confession and absolution that had virtually been lost in the Church of England since the seventeenth century. However, his advocacy of confession stirred huge controversy and opposition, since there was among Anglicans at that time a deep mistrust of practices that were thought to come from Rome.

A contemporary account by Valerie Bonham of the founding of the Community of St. John the Baptist at Clewer describes the conflict between Bishop Samuel Wilberforce and Pusey. The bishop's severe antipathy to Roman Catholic ritual led to his seeking to ban the sisters from going to Pusey for confession:

Pusey had begun hearing confessions as early as 1838 in response to requests from would-be penitents. The Book of Common Prayer clearly made provision for confessions and absolution, and the spiritual revival which the Oxford Tracts inspired made many people desire this sacrament. But many others saw it as a "Popish practice" and were especially suspicious of female penitents confessing to a priest. Pusey was careful not to seek out penitents or to encourage habitual confession, but neither did he feel able to refuse to hear confessions or to give ghostly counsel. He saw such requests as the natural outcome of a deepening awareness of sin and a natural desire to unburden the soul.[2]

In 1878, towards the end of his long life, Pusey wrote a very full introduction to his edition of Abbé Gaume's manual, which he published as *Advice for those who Exercise the Ministry of Reconciliation through Confession and Absolution.* In presenting a historical justification of the practice of hearing confessions within the Anglican tradition, he distinguishes carefully between the work of a confessor and that of a spiritual director. Pusey has very harsh words to say about the distortions spiritual direction is prone to, while he recognizes his own gifts to people as a confessor. What he commends accords very closely with the best practice in spiritual direction today; what he condemns as "direction" is what I should hope any good director would condemn also. In his own words:

People, who are in earnest about their souls, are not capricious about them: and they continue, perhaps for tens of years, to make their confessions to the same priest. They, of course, acquire, so to speak, an additional right to make them, beyond the right which every soul which has needs has towards one who has heretofore been its physician. But the priest acquires none. This is all so obvious that the only occasion for saying it is that at this time so many talk against confession. It has nothing whatever to do with priestly power, which people have learned to talk of from the bad book of a French writer.

I have never undertaken what is technically called the office of "director." Naturally I have given such spiritual advice as I could, and have answered questions whenever I have been asked them to the best of the ability which God may have given me. These of course have ranged over the whole compass of human wants, as far as I could be of use to any one, or they thought that I could be of use, theological, controversial, scriptural, moral, spiritual, practical; cases of conscience or intellectual perplexity.

I did not and could not, when it was laid upon me in the Providence of God, decline the office of guiding in what way I could by His help souls which came to me and did not willingly fail those who came to ask my help in any respect in which I could help them. But from the first moment in which people entrusted me in any degree with the care of their souls, I remember that my object was to see how God was leading them, not to lead them myself. I never interfered with any bias or choice which was not sinful. The event went oftentimes contrary to my human wishes or judgement.[3]

Pusey then quotes with approval T. T. Carter, the priest who together with Harriet Monsell was responsible for the foundation of the sisterhood at Clewer:

> Direction, rightly understood is only "ghostly counsel and advice" become habitual. The true object of direction is not to preserve a hold on the mind of the penitent and habituate it to lean on authority, overruling its own powers of action by minute details of rule, but rather to develop true principles and waken dormant energies within the soul, so as to enable it to judge and act more healthfully for itself.

It was one of Pusey's main concerns in this preface to counter the idea that spiritual direction or the ministry of a confessor was a matter of the clergy wielding power over other people. He could not countenance any kind of manipulation of those who came for confession or advice:

> I have been asked to take this opportunity of warning against "over-direction." "I wish," one writes to me, "something could be done to check the tendency on the part of some clergy to claim implicit obedience on all sorts of subjects from their penitents. Instead of trying to deepen and develop the sense of personal moral responsibility, they really crush it, and so help to justify one of the ordinary objections to the system."

> Self-assertion, or a seeming wish to gain power over the minds of others...gives at least a plausible plea for the common declamation against "priestly influence." It was well said once that "the guide of souls ought to be transparent to lead people to Christ." Our office is not to

supersede but to develop and deepen a sense of moral responsibility; to teach those who look to us for guidance how to use the judgement which God has given them; to furnish them with clear principles to discern right from wrong: to suggest to them how to discern, in the secret whispers of conscience, the voice of God the Holy Ghost...to train them to obey, not us, but Christ, the Master of both.

Finally, recognizing the pressures that are brought to bear in a time of controversy and the dangers of distortion, Pusey gives counsel to his fellow clergy that offers good insights for lay people and clergy working in spiritual direction in any age:

> We, the clergy, are not exempt from the human infirmity of love of power, which in us, as well as in the rest of our race, can only be kept down by the grace of God....It is of course flattering to human self-esteem to be consulted on all sorts of matters; so we have need to watch warily, even when walking in a right path.

Edward King

A generation younger than Pusey, Bishop Edward King is one of the pastoral saints of the Church of England: a man of marked personal holiness with a widespread reputation for the care of souls. King was principal of the theological college at Cuddesdon and professor of pastoral theology at Oxford University before becoming Bishop of Lincoln. The memorial brass to him at Cuddesdon describes him as "so blending strength with gentleness, seriousness with joyousness, love with wisdom, that all men rejoiced to recognise in him the very presence of Christ and took courage."

One of his students collected the notes of lectures King gave at Oxford in 1874. They reveal his insistence on the necessity for the pastor to be a holy person, close to Christ, and the need for real understanding of and respect for human nature. "This sort of love," he wrote, "would lead, I think, to the 'honouring of all men' without respect of persons." In a similar way King's *Spiritual Letters*, collected after his death by B.W. Randolph, reflect his warmth as well as his spirituality. The qualities that shine out from them are the loving nature of the man and his deep concern for the good of the person to whom he is writing. Many of the letters are written to ordinands and clergy, for much of his work lay in their education, training, and oversight, but there are also several to friends and acquaintances who had consulted him. The first series in the collection is an almost life-long correspondence opening in 1858 with King writing to a young man working as a teacher, and closes in 1909 with him writing:

> God bless you, dear C., and guide you on to the end, which is really the *great beginning*. Remember me in your prayers, as I do you, every day. God bless you and all like you.[4]

In between there is news and comment on all sorts of events in the life of the man and his family. Interspersed are words of spiritual counsel, often in response to questions or problems, such as that posed by the young man, now a student at teacher training college, concerning his nervousness. King writes about his own experience:

> You know I am a wretched shaky old thing frightened to death, but I try to get the better of it. I do think that perfect humility, being content to be anywhere God places one, does cure a great deal of nervousness, and so leaves one's mind more free to do its work....But come and see me, and I will finish my *sermon* then.

Writing to another young man on the eve of his ordination to the priesthood, King remembers his own ministry:

> My joy is to think that my dear and merciful Lord will take you. *Twenty* years ago tomorrow he took me in the same Church, and for *twenty years* He has put up with me, and never left me, nor let me wholly leave Him, but led me on till at least I can say, honestly, "There is none like him," and honestly I can joyfully trust that He will do for you as He has for me.

> Simply give yourself to God; never mind what you *feel*, your being weary or excited, or put out by some trifles, but that will pass and the great supernatural *fact* will remain.

In the following letter he writes to thank a priest friend for the present of a book and refers to the mutual relationships that he enjoyed in his parish and teaching work:

> For all your kind words I cannot attempt to thank you, but they are a great comfort to me, not because I deserve them (I know that), but because they convey the inestimable comfort of responsive love. At Wheatley and Cuddesdon and Oxford I enjoyed through God's unspeakable goodness such abundance of love, that the more formal life of a Bishop, I fear, does make me cold and hard and selfish.

In another, he replies to a man recently appointed to the staff of a missionary college who told King about being under pressure:

> I am sorry you are so squeezed, but it must be so, more or less. Anyone who has a high ideal and love of perfection must be prepared to suffer. I am very fond of the Prophets. Among other things they seem to have suf-

fered a great deal.... They are a great help to me. So you must not be in despair, dear friend. By degrees you will, please God, get on. I should make a quiet gentle push to get Friday Meditations. One slides away from personal piety so very easily and in so many respectable ways that unless there is a systematic consideration of the unseen spiritual life there is always danger.

Don't over worry, dear friend, and yet you must have a share in the sufferings, depression and amazements of the prophets if you are really to lead men in the way of God.

In the following year, however, the pressure seemed even more intense, and King gave him the following counsel:

Dearest, dearest thing! I am so sorry for you, and yet it *must, must* be. Oh, you would not be worth your salt in such a place. Only by breaking your poor heart into pieces over and over again can you hope to make them begin to think of believing that there is such a thing as love. How I wish I could help you, but I can only say you will never regret *all* the misery you go through: it is not lost, no, not one bit of it. Not one drop of heart's blood that falls from a love-broken heart ever gets lost; angels look after it if men don't, and it bears fruit. Trust, dear friend, and love on.

One woman had written to Bishop King for advice about a new ministry but then chose to ignore it. He replied to her letter, which is a good example of his stance as a director in giving full responsibility to the people who consulted him:

I thank you for your kind letter, though the responsibility weighs heavily upon me. Still, I offered the best contribution that I had, and I offered it as a contribution to help you to make up your own mind, and I am still of the same opinion. May God guide and bless your decision, to your own happiness and the highest good of others.

To a priest in his diocese King wrote, concerning communion with God:

Thank you for your trustful letter. I shall only be too glad and thankful if I can help you as you propose. Indeed it is my great wish, if it please God, to help on clergy of the diocese into peaceful communion with God, that they may then be enabled to do the same for their people.

When you come we will find a time for you to tell me all you wish. It is not all at once, very often, that we can attain that even and consistent living with God which in His time may be ours: and which, when attained is such a rest. That this may be yours and that you may be enabled to bring others to the same is my sincere prayer.

Some short quotations from other letters show a remarkable consistency in the comments and advice that he gave:

You must not over worry yourself about your advance in the Christian life. It is very simple, the love of God and love of man. That is perfection! Keep your heart with God, and then do the daily duties, and He will take care of you. He knows, and watches and leads us on.

Sometimes I long for rest, but I believe if one had more faith, and trusted to one's daily bread to give strength for the daily duties, one would have power enough. To be thankful in looking back over the past, and content and cheerful in the present, and trustful and hopeful in looking to the future, is what I am trying to aim at.

In the last letter King wrote to his diocese six days before his death, he looked back over his ministry:

> I fear I am not able to write the letter I should wish to write. I have for some time been praying God to tell me when I should give up my work. Now He has sent me in his loving wisdom a clear answer. It is a very great comfort to me to be relieved from the responsibility of leaving you.

> All I have to do is to ask you to forgive the many faults and shortcomings during the twenty-five years I have been with you, and to ask you to pray God to perfect my repentance and strengthen my faith to the end. All has been done in perfect love and wisdom.

> My great wish has been to lead you to be Christlike Christians. In Christ is the only true hope of unity and peace. In Him we may be united to God and to one another. May God guide and bless you all and refresh you with the increasing consciousness of His Presence and His Love.

Anglican Sisterhoods

It should not be thought that nineteenth-century religious movements were the sole preserve of the clergy, because one important aspect of the Oxford Movement was the renewal of interest in the religious life in the Church of England. In particular this period is remarkable for its large number of communities of women, many of them formed to meet the clamoring social needs of the day. The list of women who led these sisterhoods includes Marion Rebecca Hughes, of the Oxford Convent of the Holy Trinity, the first to be professed, whose vows Pusey received in 1841, and Priscilla Lydia Sellon, who founded the Society of the Holy Trinity at Devonport. These two women and many others were notable for their leadership of the new sisterhoods and for their wise care both of the women who joined as religious and of the needy people who looked to them for help. Their advice was also in some demand, for both men and women looked to them as having a recognized spiritual authority as well as personal strength.

Since childhood Emily Ayckbowm felt she had been called to help the poor, a call that developed into her fixed intention to give herself up altogether to God's service. After her father's death she continued to work among the poor of his parish in Chester for some years before moving to London to found the Church Extension Association. Out of this grew the Community of the Sisters of the Church. As superior of the community, Ayckbowm inspired and organized a huge amount of activity to meet the needs of the poverty-stricken and the outcast. She founded schools for poor children, orphanages, convalescent homes, and night refuges, together with hostels and restaurants for the working poor and the unemployed in the slums of London. For the sisterhood she wrote a rule of life that is evidence of her strong, clear common sense and wisdom as well as her dedication to prayer. Soon after she died in 1900, a clergyman who knew her intimately said to the sorrowing sisters:

> One of God's great souls has founded a great work, has drawn up a noble Rule, a grand conception of a Religious Order. Keep this in the power of the Holy Ghost; hand it on unimpaired, hand on the true traditions of the Foundress.

Only those who knew our foundress well can realise what an inspiring thing a talk with her could be. The most timid workers would feel their hearts stirred to courage by her words and looks. The sisters have a thousand happy memories of conferences and consultations with her, which would send them back to their work, their hearts on fire for fresh effort, more devoted service, greater self sacrifice in their Master's cause, and for His poor. Even outsiders who knew her but slightly, felt her strong influence, and were deeply impressed by her personality.

His sentiments are echoed by a woman who wrote of Ayckbowm:

I only once had the pleasure of meeting your Mother Superior and that was twenty years ago, but I have never forgotten the impression she made on me. She was the first who helped me to understand what is meant by "the Beauty of Holiness."[5]

Another leading figure of the period, Harriet Monsell, was the daughter of an Anglo-Irish family. She married Charles Monsell, who was ordained shortly after their marriage but died young of consumption in 1850. Harriet Monsell was well connected to prominent families in England, including that of William Ewart Gladstone, the liberal statesman and prime minister, and of the Archbishop of Canterbury. Monsell's life task began when she took over a ministry that had already been started among prostitutes at Clewer near Windsor. In 1852 she was professed and appointed superior of an Anglican sisterhood, the Community of St. John the Baptist, which under her leadership became the largest sisterhood in the Church of England.

She resigned as superior in 1875 because of failing health, and died in 1883.

Queen Victoria visited the community at Clewer and noted afterwards, "Mrs. Monsell, the Mother Superior, is an excellent person and manages the whole admirably." Monsell was not only a gifted manager of the work and of the resources it demanded, but also profoundly spiritual and deeply involved in the life of the members of the community. Letters show the care with which she encouraged their development as religious and as individuals. As A. M. Allchin writes, "With her strength of character, firmness of faith, an infectious sense of humour, a gift for listening, and a magnetism that none could resist, Harriet Monsell was one of the greatest women of her day."[6]

Monsell's own notes on qualities required by a religious give an idea both of the spirituality of her direction and her leadership:

> Of the inner life: to live alone with God, wholly satisfied in God, silent in God, seeking rest in a life of loneliness with God, drawn off from others into an inner life concentrated on God. A life of silent adoration, of active obedience, of conformity to the Will of God, a life dead to self that Christ may live in you.

The sisters of Clewer were to be women who, in the words of Harriet Monsell, "sometimes had to be ready to leave God for God, to leave God in devotion to work for God in those for whom he shed His blood." T. T. Carter, cofounder of the community, wrote that Monsell

> impressed all with her wisdom, her grand mind, the power she had of sympathising wit, and understanding all kinds of different minds, and her *delight* in doing so. She shewed in all she said a thorough knowledge of the

World *and* (as it seemed to one outside) the highest idea of the Religious Life. One thing that was felt to be so great a charm in her was the combination of extreme tenderness with a strong character, and although so many leant upon her and confided in her it was impossible not to be struck with her entire absence of self consciousness and her great personal humility. . . . Very few words from her would seem full of meaning, would leave a lasting impression. [7]

The early story of another religious community founded in the nineteenth century, the Community of St. Mary the Virgin at Wantage, indicates the strong partnership between William John Butler, the founder, and Mother Harriet. Diffident in the early stages of her time as superior, she grew into someone who was able to meet the demands of women flocking to test their vocation as well as the oversight of the community and its work. In her contact with a wide cross-section of people she would have had opportunity for guiding them, even if unobtrusively. The term "counseling" was not used in those days, nor was "spiritual direction;" it was called simply "talking to people" and had a definite aim. Butler, the community's founder, was also described as "desirous of training souls" and respecting the individuality of each one. He allowed, it was said, "scope for the enthusiasm of the young and ardent, while he controlled and directed it. In all that he counselled and ordered he himself set an example." After Butler's death, Edward King wrote of how he had "striven to win souls for Christ" and, at the end, "resigned all that mysterious spiritual work in which for so many years he had been ceaselessly engaged."[8]

By now anyone who is aware of the different dimensions of the Church of England knows that its tradition of spiritual direction is mainly to be found in its more catholic wing. We have seen that many of the Caroline divines are set firmly within the Anglican middle way and hold to the best of both the Roman Catholic and the Reformed inheritance. But the theologians I have cited tended to be creatively conservative, still valuing what they judged to be best from the past, which meant that they were not in favour with more extreme reformers. Jeremy Taylor was forced to live in internal exile during the Commonwealth period, while Thomas Ken and William Law placed themselves outside the main stream of the church as Non-Jurors.

As the catholic emphasis gained strength with the Oxford Movement, the strong interest in the history of the church and a respect for the wisdom of the past were renewed. The Tractarians looked back to the Anglican writers of the sixteenth and seventeenth centuries and beyond them to the patristic period and the theologians of the early church. In the particular area of spiritual guidance they were willing to look to teachers in the Roman Catholic tradition. Nor was this true only for the nineteenth century: it would be fascinating to list the number of times that Thomas à Kempis and his *Imitation of Christ* appears as a resource for Anglicans over the centuries. And he is not alone: spiritual teachers like Fénelon, St. François de Sales, and Jean Pierre de Caussade, together with St. Ignatius of Loyola and the Carmelites Teresa of Avila and John of the Cross, were all accepted as valuable guides on the spiritual journey.

The close link between spiritual direction and sacramental confession also arose with the Oxford Movement and has continued to mark the tradition of the Church of England. With the development of counselling as a ministry within the church and with the growth in the number of lay directors this link has become weaker over the last decades of this century.

Endnotes

1. Extracts from John Keble's letters are from the 1870 edition of his *Letters of Spiritual Counsel* (Parker, London).

2. Valerie Bonham, *A Place in Life: The Clewer House of Mercy 1849-83* (Valerie Bonham and the Community of St. John the Baptist, 1992), 104.

3. Extracts from Edward Bouverie Pusey are from the 1878 edition of his *Advice for those who Exercise the Ministry of Reconciliation through Confession and Absolution* (Parker, London).

4. Selections from Edward King's letters are from the 1910 edition of *The Spiritual Letters of Edward King, D.D.*, published in London and Oxford by Mowbray.

5. Anonymous, *Some memories of Emily Harriet Ayckbowm, Mother Foundress of the Community of the Sisters of the Church* (London: Church Extension Association, 1914), from the preface.

6. Quoted in Bonham, *A Place in Life*, 281-82.

7. *Ibid.*, 245.

8. Quoted by Sister Hilary, CSMV in a letter to the author.

Chapter 4

Evangelicals and the Spiritual Life

From the early days of the Reformation and the time of the settlement under Elizabeth I, the Church of England has encompassed a mixture of traditions. Because of this diversity, to look at the tradition of spiritual direction simply from one angle is to distort it. So it is important to give consideration to another aspect of Anglican worship and practice, which is the evangelical tradition. The way the English use the word "evangelical" differs from its use on the continent of Europe. In Germany the churches that stem from the Reformation tend to be known as evangelical, whether they are Lutheran or Calvinist. In Switzerland, however, evangelical is restricted to Lutheran churches; Calvinist churches there are described as reformed. In England, evangelical also has a particular meaning.

The roots of evangelicalism lie in the early days of the Reformation and before. Puritan divines like Thomas Cartwright, an important leader of the cause in the sixteenth century, and John Owen, who was dean of Christ Church in Oxford under Cromwell, looked to the scriptures in order to justify church decisions and aspects of public worship. In many cases these Puritans were in conflict with the Church of England for their strong Calvinist position and looked to Presbyterianism or Independency (Congregationalism).

The evangelical revival of the mid-eighteenth century brought new impetus. Its keynote was its immediacy. Growing out of and as a reaction to the rational religion of the Enlightenment, the religious revival stressed four things. From the first evangelicals proclaimed the vital necessity of personal conversion, their conviction that lives must be changed by a personal encounter with Christ. They expect conversion to be followed by a commitment to a life of energetic service for the gospel, particularly in evangelism; the Christian is to be active in prayer, mission, and service in the world. They are deeply concerned to uphold the primacy and authority of the scriptures and the Bible as being available to all. For them the cross of Christ is at the heart of salvation; they have supreme confidence in the power of the cross and its centrality both to the gospel and to Christian discipleship.[1]

From the start evangelical religion has been a religion of revival. The shape of its history is like a series of ocean waves. Successive waves of revival are usually associated with an individual or a small group of enthusiasts, sometimes English and Anglican, sometimes Nonconformist or from overseas. Revivals are marked by periods of intense activity, often centered on an individual leader or on a group of dedicated individuals and their rediscovery of the Bible as their guide for faith and life. With the death of these leaders, the pressure of activity tends to diminish. The motive power of the revival and its deep sense of fellowship tend to fade towards a more settled church existence with the passing of the first generation.

This emphasis on revival and the insistence on the immediacy of the gospel to people's lives means that evangelicals make far less appeal than catholics do to the authority of the church's past. Instead, their main appeal is to the Bible, especially to the letters of St. Paul, and to the evidence of God at work changing lives in the present. There certainly are heroes from the past, but their attraction fades in comparison with living heroes, the witness of whose stories underlines the power of the gospel today.

The seventeenth century was not solely the theological preserve of the Caroline divines, whom we discussed earlier, for there were influential Puritan divines as well. Richard Baxter, whose life spanned the greater part of the seventeenth century, ministered both within and without the Church of England, chiefly in the parish church of Kidderminster. Baxter was a champion of moderation who, both in his Puritan stance and his devotion to the established church, believed in a moderate episcopacy and an ordered liturgy. As he wrote in his manual for ministers, *The Reformed Pastor:*

> We have as sad divisions among us in England, considering the piety of the persons and the smallness of the matter of our discord, as most nations under heaven have known. The most that keeps us at odds is but about the right form and order of church government. Is the distance so great that Presbyterian, Episcopal and Independent might not be well agreed? Were they but heartily willing and forward for peace, they might—I know they might....Ministers must smart when the Church is wounded, and be so far from being the leaders in divisions, that they should take it as a principal part of their work to prevent and heal them.[2]

In keeping with this belief Baxter tried to take a middle road between extremes, and suffered from both. His writing reveals a man who is a mixture of deep compassion and firm didacticism, with strong pastoral concern for individuals and a clear offer of gospel truths for their improvement and their good. He developed a system of group meetings for local ministers to help them grow in their devotion and skills. Baxter's devotional classic, *The Saints' Everlasting Rest,* as well as *The Reformed Pastor,* can take their place with the writings of Ken Thomas and Jeremy Taylor. Writing about "the oversight of the flock," Baxter encourages the parish minister in his duty to labor for the conversion of the unconverted, ready to give advice to those who come to him with cases of conscience, and build up those who are already truly converted, including

> many of our flock that are weak, who, though they are of long standing, are yet of small proficiency and strength. And indeed it is the most common condition of the godly. Many of them stick in low degrees of grace and it is no easy matter to get them higher.

> Another sort of converts that need our help, are those that labor under some particular distemper that keeps under their graces and maketh them temptations and troubles to others.... It is our duty to set in for the assistance of all these; and partly by dissuasions and clear discoveries of the odiousness of their sin, and partly by suitable directions about the way of remedy, to help them to a more complete conquest of their corruptions.

In a similar vein of clear spiritual direction, Baxter goes on to describe ways of working with "declining Christians that are either fallen into some scandalous sin or else abate their zeal and diligence, and show us that they have lost their former love" together with the tempted and the disconsolate. He concludes:

> The rest of our ministerial work is upon those that are yet strong, for they also have need of our assistance: partly to prevent their temptations and declinings and

preserve the grace they have; and partly to help them for a further progress and increase of their strength in the service of Christ and the assistance of their brethren.

His remarks on the importance of pastoral care for families would do justice to a contemporary campaigner for "family values," insisting that

> we must also have a special eye upon families, to see that they be well ordered, and the duties of each relation performed. The life of religion and the welfare and glory of Church and State, dependeth much on family government and duty.[3]

In some ways the evangelical revival can be seen as developing out of the Puritan wing of the Reformation, but in its intensity and the freshness of its effect it has to be recognized as something new to the church in England. Key figures in the revival are John Wesley, his brother Charles, George Whitefield, and John Newton. The Wesleys and Whitefield were together in the "Holy Club" at Oxford. Afterwards the brothers invited Whitefield to join them in America, working among the British colonists in Georgia, but the Wesleys had returned to England before he arrived.

While still in the colonies, John Wesley's agonized search for genuine religious faith and commitment brought him into contact with the Moravian sect, Lutherans who believed in a religion of the heart in contrast to the arid intellectualism and moral concern of contemporary Lutheranism. John Wesley first met them in Georgia and later visited their center at Herrnhut, preparing the way for his profound experience of conversion in 1738. His teaching and the hymns of both Wesleys reflect the central importance of the Christian's assurance of salvation that flowed from their experience of conversion. Following his conversion John Wesley began evangelistic preaching throughout the country and in America. Anglican churches were closed to him, so he preached first to open-air gatherings and later in chapels built by local Methodist societies. It was his ordaining ministers in America that led to the eventual split between the Methodists and Anglicans, although both he and his brother always remained Anglican priests.

Alongside the doctrine of assurance, which has had so much influence on Methodism, lies the concept of holiness. Methodism taught the pursuit of holiness as the way of life to be sought, and the system of "class meetings" was designed to promote piety among the members of the societies.

The pursuit of holiness was also an important emphasis among a significant group of people in the early nineteenth century who came to be known as the Clapham Sect, named after their meetings in the house of Henry Venn, the rector of Clapham and one of the founders of the Church Missionary Society. These wealthy and influential evangelical Christians worked actively for the improvement of society. William Wilberforce, perhaps the most famous member, was the leading voice against the slave trade and helped achieve its abolition. The group was also responsible for the founding of the British and Foreign Bible Society and for the development of missionary activity at home and abroad, especially in India.

Later nineteenth-century evangelicals included powerful figures like Charles Spurgeon, a prominent Baptist preacher, the Americans Ira Sankey and Dwight Moody. These two men spent several years on evangelistic tours in Britain. Their book of hymns and songs was published in 1873 to provide material more suitable for singing in revivalist rallies than could be found in the church hymn books of the day. As vicar of Holy Trinity, Cambridge, furthermore, Charles Simeon augmented his preaching ministry with what he called "conversation classes," inviting undergraduates, particularly those studying theology in preparation for ordination, to meet at his home and talk about their faith.

The pentecostal movement began in America in the early years of the twentieth-century, but at that time had only limited effect on the Church of England. Similarly, the East African revival, which brought new life and vigor to the Anglican church in Uganda and neighboring territories, had only a small impact in Britain. However, an important landmark in the contemporary story of revival is the series of missions led by Billy Graham beginning in the middle of the century, followed by the the impact of the charismatic renewal that has been a strong feature in the life of the churches since the 1960s.

In this quick sketch of evangelicalism it becomes apparent that, in contrast to the catholic and broad church Anglicans we discussed earlier, who influenced spiritual direction through their quiet counseling of individuals, the important evangelical figures tend to be famous preachers and other people in the public eye. It also seems that, just as the catholic stream in the Church of England has been strongly influenced by individuals and movements from other countries and churches, particularly Roman Catholics and Russian and Greek Orthodox churches, evangelicals have also been open to outside sources. They have found fellowship with members and groups in other denominations that share their central concerns. Instead of John of the Cross, Teresa of Avila, and Ignatius of Loyola in Spain, Francis de Sales and Jean Pierre de Caussade in France, evangelical influences are likely to be Free Church, often Baptist, and to come from the United States.

Important as they are, we should not concentrate only on the work of these leading evangelical figures, the preachers, teachers, and writers. We need also to recognize that much of the movement's strength comes from its popular roots. The great characteristic of evangelical devotion is the Quiet Time, the hour spent daily reading and meditating on the Bible. It is seen as vital and stretches back in an unbroken line of tradition. As one observer writes:

> Popular devotional aids are another resource when seeking to put one's finger on the pulse of evangelical spirituality within a particular period and cultural setting. These are the books, tracts, daily readings, magazines, pictures, music cassettes and what might be called the minor accessories of the tradition—stickers, lapel badges, Bible markers, greetings cards, etc. These often give a more accurate picture of a people's spirituality than do the books of its leaders.[4]

Evangelical Spiritual Direction

First it is worth making the point that, until very recently, the title I have given to this section would not have found favor in evangelical circles. This is not to say that spiritual direction did not exist in other forms, nor that evangelicals were not or are not concerned for growth in Christian discipleship, deepening in prayer, or a life based on faith. Far from it. Richard Baxter urged the pastor to catechize from house to house, which for him would have meant urging people towards holiness—a form of spiritual direction. Each successive revival has looked for individual conversions with an urgency often lacking in other branches of the church.

Following conversion, evangelicals have consistently urged people towards radical personal change, giving themselves to active prayer and to an active service for the Lord that involves both evangelism and meeting the needs of others. A good example is John Newton, a slave-trading sea captain who converted to Christianity and became a priest, evangelist, and hymn writer. Newton wrote his own epitaph in his church of St. Mary Woolnoth in the City of London:

> JOHN NEWTON, Clerk, once an infidel and libertine, a servant of slaves in Africa, was by the rich mercy of our Lord and Saviour Jesus Christ, preserved, restored, pardoned and appointed to preach the Faith he had long laboured to destroy. Near sixteen years at Olney in Bucks; and twenty-seven years in this Church.

It was while he was at Olney that Newton worked with the poet William Cowper to produce hymns for the weekly prayer meeting in the parish, hymns such as "Amazing Grace" and "O for a closer walk with God."

Newton's book *Cardiphonia*, which consists of actual letters written to his friends, gives a vivid picture of the man. His letters sound more like devotional addresses than spiritual direction because they are not necessarily in reply to questions asked by the correspondents. Still, the correspondence deals with the problems that face a Christian in growing in faith and obedience. The book is full of comfort to the afflicted and the tempted, along with Newton's firm belief that God is in the details of individual life. Throughout there is the evangelical insistence on the saving love of God:

> O the comfort, we are not under law but under grace. The Gospel is a dispensation for sinners, and we have an Advocate with the Father. There is the unshaken ground of hope; a reconciled Father, a prevailing Advocate, a

powerful Shepherd, a compassionate Friend, a Savior, who is able and willing to save to the uttermost. He knows our frame; he remembers that we are but dust, and has opened for us a new and blood-besprinkled way of access to the throne of grace that we may obtain mercy and find grace to help in every time of need.

Furthermore, his writing is not without insight and wit, which is nowhere more evident than in his remarks about the over-zealousness of new converts:

The awakened soul...finds itself as in a new world. The transition from darkness to light, from a sense of wrath to a hope of glory, is the greatest that can be imagined....Hence the general characteristics of young converts are zeal and love....They have just seen the wonderful works of the Lord, and they cannot but sing his praise; they are deeply affected with the danger they have lately escaped, and with the case of the multitudes around them, who are secure and careless in the same alarming situation; and a sense of their own mercies, and a compassion for the souls of others, is so transporting that they can hardly forbear preaching to everyone they meet.

The emotion is highly just and reasonable with respect to the causes from which it springs...yet it is not entirely genuine.

1. Such persons are very weak in faith. Their confidence arises rather from the lively impressions of joy, than from a distinct and clear apprehension of the work of God in Christ. The comforts which are intended as cordials to animate them against the opposition of an unbelieving world, they mistake and rest in as proper evidences of their hope. And hence it comes to pass, that

when the Lord varies his dispensations, and hides his face, they are soon troubled and at their wits end.

2. They who are in this state of their first love, are seldom free from something of a censorious spirit. They have not yet felt all the deceitfulness of their own hearts; they are not well acquainted with the devices or temptations of Satan; and therefore know not how to sympathise or make allowances, where allowances are necessary and due, and can hardly bear with any who do not discover the same earnestness as themselves.

They are likewise more or less under the influence of self-righteousness and self-will. They mean well; but not being as yet well acquainted with the spiritual meaning, and proper use of the law, nor established in the life of faith, a part (oftentimes a very considerable part) of their zeal spends itself in externals and non-essentials, prompts them to practise what is not commanded, to refrain from what is lawful, and to observe various and needless austerities and singularities, as their tempers and circumstances differ.

However, with all their faults, methinks there is something very beautiful and engaging in the honest vehemence of a young convert.

In another letter, with words that will resonate with the experiences of many spiritual directors, Newton describes spending time visiting a hospital. He uses the analogy of physicians who, while they have a common knowledge of their profession, also each have their special branches of study:

For myself, if it be lawful to speak of myself, and so far as I can judge, anatomy is my favourite branch; I mean the study of the human heart, with its working and counterworking, as it is differently affected by seasons of prosperity, adversity, conviction, temptation, sickness, and the approach of death.[5]

This religion of the "twice-born" is deeply personal and inward. It has at its heart the individual's own assurance of salvation, but it is also an activist view of faith. The assurance is that God has done all that is necessary; the Christian's response is to get on with the active service that is the duty owed to God. Sometimes this degree of activism risks a certain lack of reflectiveness among evangelicals, both in the area of doctrine and spirituality, and I have heard the evangelical way described as more a spirituality of arrival than one of journey. This is not the whole picture; as one commentator notes:

In the evangelical tradition there has often been a great tradition of spiritual guidance through friendship, fellowship groups, and sometimes, most significantly, through a ministry of letter writing. But for most the interpretation has come from the sermon (which for many fulfils the role others would look for in a spiritual director), and this, inevitably, can give no specific allowance for individual diagnosis and prescription.[6]

With individual once-for-all conversion so firmly emphasized, however, there is little sense of a gradually unfolding discovery of God. Instead, Jesus Christ makes himself fully known in conversion.

Some words from Florence Allshorn, a twentieth-century missionary, may illustrate the importance of friendship in evangelical spirituality. The Church Missionary Society is one of the lasting foundations of the early evangelical revival. As a young woman Florence Allshorn went to Uganda as a missionary for the society and was posted to a remote station with a very difficult senior colleague. Allshorn's predecessors had been unable to stay with her, but with the help of prayer and a daily reading of 1 Corinthians 13 she was enabled to work her full tour of duty. Later she wrote:

> To love a human being means to accept him, to love him as he is. If you wait to love him till he has got rid of his faults, till he is different, you are only loving an idea. I can only love a person by allowing myself to be disturbed by him as he is. I must accept the pain of seeing him with hopefulness and expectancy that he can be different. To love him with the love of Christ means first of all to accept him as he is, and then try to lead him towards a goal he doesn't see yet.[7]

Christian Unions

Around the time of the Second World War there began a peculiarly English manifestation of evangelical Christianity that has had a lasting effect on the Church of England. For many years camps for young men and boys have been held at Iwerne Minster in Dorset, mostly from the universities and public (independent) schools. The founder was the Rev. E. Nash, and the goal Christian conversion against a background friendship and warmth in a hospitable atmosphere, modelled on the social expectations of the boys. These camps have changed greatly over the years, but the core commitment to a devotional and applied reading of Scripture and a theological focus on the person of Christ and Jesus as friend have been constant. Many men, both ordained and lay, who are leading figures in the church today came to faith through these camps.

Without these middle class overtones, the same urge to convert can be found in school and university Christian Unions, a movement stressing the Christian's duty to lead others to Christ through witness and through friendship.The methods may be more prescriptive than many people's idea of spiritual direction, but I was struck by the similarities as I read over some old notes prepared by a Christian Union to help students accompany new converts. They stress that God's will is that each should be sanctified, not just justified, and urge that the approach should be prayerful, humble, by example, and selfless.

Imagine that someone has just professed faith in Christ. He may be rejoicing at what he has done or he may already have doubts as to whether anything real has happened. How can we help him? He needs to understand what has happened. So go over the steps of becoming a Christian simply. "Admit your need. Believe that Christ died for you. Come to Him." Show him that it is possible to have assurance. Explain the part that feelings play. Remember that we must trust Christ's promises, not feelings.

He needs to know what happens when he sins. Being "born again" into the family of God is irreversible. So when he sins the relationship isn't broken; but it is spoilt. It is restored when he claims and acts upon a promise like 1 John 1:9.

He needs to know how to grow in the Christian life. This includes fellowship. Take him to a few selected meetings. It is probably most important that he should continue to go to the Sunday evening sermons. Introduce him to your Christian friends. In one sense on becoming a Christian he will not be able to remain quite so close to his old friends, so these must be replaced.

Perhaps it is our main aim to see him well established in his personal waiting upon the Lord in his Quiet Time. His friendship with Christ will be developed as he spends time speaking to Christ in prayer and letting Christ speak to him through the Bible. Fix a regular meeting with him. This is most important for no quantity of group meetings can be a substitute for this personal help. You will be able to deal with some of the questions raised later on, but more important you will be able to teach him how by reading the Bible he can feed on Christ. [8]

Sanctification and Holiness

Sanctification, the pursuit of holiness, is deeply ingrained in the evangelical way of being a Christian. It is seen in the tradition of time given regularly to reading the Bible and prayer, which leads to sacrificial self-giving in the service of Christ crucified. The stories of countless men and women can be called in evidence to show the power of this way of being a Christian. To explore in more detail the principles and practice of spiritual direction in the evangelical tradition, we need first to recognize that holiness is a central evangelical concept. It is the work of the Holy Spirit effecting change throughout a person's life and comes through deep attention to the scriptures and prayer. It is not something that human effort can achieve, yet it is possible for people to help one another in achieving holiness.

The Reformation principle that there is no need of any mediator between God and human beings other than Jesus Christ has been strong throughout the evangelical story. Every man, woman, and child has their own direct access to God. This means that nothing must be done that would suggest that they have need for any intermediary. The office of the preacher and teacher is to ensure that people have a clear understanding of the gospel so that they have the freedom to hear and to follow God's call. In this way it is to the great preachers in the tradition that we have to look for signs of spiritual direction. This was probably even truer in previous generations when there was more general respect for authority in society at large. Preachers should not be thought of as in any sense intermediaries in the relationship between people and God; it is the hearer's own personal responsibility to apply to his or her own situation the universal word of God as presented by the preacher.

> The evangelical approach to religion is that our freedom of access to God, the availability and comprehensibility of the scriptures to all, and the priesthood of all believers render unnecessary all reliance on systems and special intermediaries to foster growth in the spiritual life. As Christianity is, in essence, a personal relationship between the individual and God, growth occurs naturally and uniquely in so far as the person remains open to the work of the Spirit of God within his or her life.[9]

The gospel of grace available to each person and the priesthood of all believers has meant that evangelicals have always valued the gifts of spiritual friendship. That is why the prayer meeting was until recently more important than the meeting for Bible study, meetings specifically designed to enable people to grow in holiness through meeting with their fellow Christians. In many Anglican churches today people are encouraged to work with prayer partners.

It is clear from my own and other people's experience that evangelical Christians are much more willing nowadays than in the past, recent as well as distant, to seek out someone for help in spiritual direction. I think there may be two possible reasons for this change. One is the general warming of the ecumenical climate and the other is the growth in confidence among evangelicals themselves. In many, though by no means all, church circles, barriers have come down and Christians of different denominations quite naturally look across boundaries for fellowship and encouragement. From being a minority in the church with somewhat of a siege mentality, Anglican evangelicals can now see themselves as arriving at a position of strength, both in numbers and influence.

We have seen that there is little tradition of personal direction in evangelism. This has meant that when evangelicals have recognized their need for help, they have looked for directors from other traditions. Many have been surprised to find that their own theological positions have been respected, although others have found that it is not easy in practice to receive spiritual direction from people who do not share their belief in assurance or from people who do not hold the same moral stance as they do.

One evangelical author has played a large part in opening people's eyes to a wider Christian tradition: American Quaker, Richard Foster. In his *Celebration of Discipline* Foster presents his understanding of the traditional spiritual disciplines of the church, both Roman Catholic and Protestant, in a way that is immediately accessible to evangelicals. In the chapter called "The Discipline of Guidance," after a description of guidance within the group of believers and contemporary illustration, Foster commends the work of the spiritual director:

> In the Middle Ages not even the greatest saints attempted the depths of the inward journey without the

help of a spiritual director. Today the concept is hardly understood, let alone practiced, except in the Catholic monastic system. That is a tragedy, for the idea of the spiritual director is highly applicable to the contemporary scene. It is a beautiful expression of divine guidance through the help of our brothers and sisters.

Then, after a brief look at the practice of spiritual direction in the time of the desert fathers and later, he describes how he sees the work of a director:

His direction is simply and clearly to lead us to our real Director. He is the means of God to open the path to the inward teaching of the Holy Spirit.

His function is purely charismatic. He leads only by the force of his own personal holiness. He is not a superior or some ecclesiastically appointed authority. The relationship is of an advisor to a friend. Though the director has obviously advanced further into the inner depths, the two are together learning and growing in the realm of the Spirit.

Against the impression that spiritual direction is narrowly limited to "spiritual" matters, Foster asserts:

Spiritual direction is concerned with the whole person and the interrelationship of all life. It is first born out of natural, spontaneous human relationships. The ordinary kinds of caring and sharing that belong to the Christian community are the starting point for spiritual direction. Out of them will flow "Kingdom authority" through mutual subordination and servanthood. A spiritual director must himself or herself be on the inward journey and be willing to share their own struggles and doubts. There needs to be a realization that together they are learning from Jesus, their present Teacher.[10]

It is a sign of grace not only that many evangelicals both use and work in spiritual direction, but that it is often to the way of St. Ignatius and to Jesuit spirituality that they look. The Scripture-based way of accompanying people through the spiritual exercises speaks to those for whom the authority of the Bible is so fundamentally important.

Endnotes

1. See David Bebbington, *Evangelicalism in Modern Britain* (London: Unwin Hyman, 1989), 5-17.

2. Richard Baxter, *The Reformed Pastor*, ed. Hugh Martin (London: SCM Press, 1956), 78.

3. *Ibid.*, 53ff.

4. David Gillett, *Trust and Obey: Explorations in Evangelical Spirituality* (London: Darton, Longman & Todd, 1993), 22.

5. John Newton, *Collected Letters*, ed. Halcyon Backhouse (London: Hodder & Stoughton, 1989), 75; 49; 91.

6. Gillett, *Trust and Obey*, 83.

7. J. H. Oldham, *Florence Allshorn and the Story of St. Julians* (London: SCM Press, 1951), 29.

8. Michael Vasey in a letter to the author.

9. Oldham, *Florence Allshorn*, 2.

10. Richard Foster, *Celebration of Discipline* (San Francisco: Harper, 1980), 159-160.

Chapter 5

Early Twentieth-Century Anglicans

The closing years of the twentieth century are marked by a proliferation of different sorts of spiritualities, some of them lumped together under the heading of New Age. A hundred years ago there was a similar interest in things of the spirit. Sometimes this took the riskier form of spiritualism, occult practices, or the search for mystical experiences through drugs; again, it was not so different from today. On other occasions people recognized that in Christian tradition there was both a past and present emphasis on relating to God in prayer, an interest reflected in the number of important books on the subject. William Inge, later to become Dean of St. Paul's, published his Oxford University Bampton Lectures in 1899 under the title *Christian Mysticism*. After beginning his lectures by stating that no word in our language, not even the term socialism, has been employed more loosely than "mysticism," Inge offers this definition: "The attempt to realize, in thought and feeling, the immanence of the temporal in the eternal and of the eternal in the temporal."[1]

Inge's work offers a careful study of mysticism in the Bible, Christian Platonism, and the leading mystical writers of the Middle Ages and later centuries. Of similar importance were William James's *Varieties of Religious Experience*, published in 1902, and Baron Friedrich von Hügel's *The Mystical Element in Religion* of 1908. Born in 1852, the son of an Austrian nobleman and a mother who had been raised as a Scottish Presbyterian, von Hügel was a liberal Roman Catholic lay theologian and philosopher whose writing and personal work had great influence in England, where he lived during most of his life.

Evelyn Underhill

Among those who were engaged in research in this area was Evelyn Underhill, a woman who was later to be described as "spiritual director to her generation." No study of spiritual direction in the Church of England could be complete without some account of her life and work. Born into a professional family and educated at King's College, London, she began as a writer of novels but in her twenties began to explore philosophy and the world of the spirit. This exploration led her at the time towards occultism; for a while she was a member of a cult known as the Hermetic Society of the Golden Dawn.

Underhill's search for mystical experience took her from atheism to conversion to Christianity at the age of thirty-two. She received help from spiritual companions and especially from Baron von Hügel, who was her friend for ten years, from 1911, and then her spiritual director until his death in 1925. She wrote her best-known work, *Mysticism*, in 1911, when her viewpoint was that of a convinced Christian, albeit without belonging to a church. Although she had thought seriously about becoming a Roman Catholic, the controversy over the modernist movement and its suppression convinced her that this route was not for her, and Underhill formally became a practicing member of the Church of England in 1921. She was someone for whom membership in the Church of England was a matter of definite personal choice, as she wrote to Dom John Chapman, who was for some time her director:

> I solidly believe in the Catholic status of the Anglican Church as to orders and sacraments, little as I appreciate many of the things done among us....The whole point to me is that our Lord has put me here, keeps on giving me more and more jobs to do for souls here, and has never given me orders to move. I know what the push of God is like, and should obey it if it came...at least I trust and believe so.[2]

Her biographer, Dana Greene, summarizes Evelyn Underhill's gifts and work in this way:

> Whether exploring the lives and writings of the mystics or detailing the spiritual life as participated in by ordinary people, her search was for the holy.

> If Underhill had merely examined the phenomenon of mysticism and the lives of the mystics, her contribution would have been considerable: however, she did more than this. In the last fifteen years of her life she explored the spiritual life as lived out by ordinary men and women. As a retreat director, spiritual guide, and writer on the spiritual life, she offered her contemporaries her counsel, inspiration, and encouragement.[3]

Underhill wanted people to be aware of God as reality. Through books and articles, retreats, and giving spiritual direction both in personal meetings and in letters, she shared her wide learning and her sense of vision. Olive Wyon, a friend and colleague who wrote a number of very well-received books on prayer around the time of the Second World War, describes her way with people:

> One young woman who went to see her says she can never forget the way Evelyn *listened*. It was a winter afternoon; gradually the light faded, and still the two sat on in the light of the fire; the house was absolutely quiet, and Evelyn listened, as this girl had never been listened to before; there was a sense of being utterly understood. When Evelyn spoke, at the end, her few words were wise and quiet, and she followed the talk with a letter of direction that was invaluable in its wisdom and understanding.

She also had a strong sense of compassion, which is well illustrated in the long series of letters that she wrote to her friend Lucy Menzies, warden of Underhill's much loved retreat house at Pleshey. She saw her role as a helper in discernment and a source of balance in the lives of those whom she directed, such as when she insists that Lucy Menzies take care of herself properly:

> Take *special* pains now to keep up fully or develop some definite non-religious interests, e.g. your music. Work at it, consider it an obligation to do so. It is more necessary to your spiritual health and you will very soon find that it has a steadying effect.... If you could take a few days off and keep quite quiet it would be good, but if this is impossible, at any rate go along gently, look after your body, don't saturate yourself the whole time with mystical books....Hot milk and a thoroughly foolish novel are better things for you to go to bed on just now than St. Teresa.

Besides her compassion and sense of balance, the other gifts that Evelyn Underhill brought to spiritual direction were her strong scholarship and her spiritual experience. Her own life was a quest for God in which periods of darkness did not destroy her desire to find out more, and she used this positively in her dealing with others. She had experienced as well as studied and she loved to teach. In her writings she frequently uses the words "vision" and "reality." In a lecture to teachers she told her audience:

The most important thing for you is your vision, your sense of that God whom your work must glorify. The richer, deeper, wider, truer your vision of Divine Reality the more real, rich and fruitful your work is going to be. You must feel the mysterious attraction of God, His loveliness and wonder, if you are ever going—in however simple a way—to impart it to others.[4]

A theologian and contemporary of Underhill's, Charles Williams, quotes her own account of coming to faith in the introduction to his edition of her letters:

For some time I remained predominantly theocentric. But…more and more my whole religious life and experience seem to centre with increasing vividness on our Lord—that sort of quasi-involuntary prayer that springs up of itself at odd moments is always now directed to Him. . . . Holy Communion which at first I did simply under obedience, gets more and more wonderful too. It's in that world and atmosphere one lives.[5]

Underhill's whole life was one of searching for the reality. In this she had the help of several outstanding directors, the Roman Catholics Dom John Chapman and Baron von Hügel, the Anglicans Bishop Frere and, in the later part of her life, Reginald Somerset Ward. Her biographer describes their work together:

It was within the context of Anglicanism and with the help of Anglican directors that Underhill was sustained in her demanding work and helped to confront the inner turmoil that afflicted her for years. Her external serenity, obvious in her person and her writing, was not matched in her inner life.... Ward helped her deal with self-preoccupation and its consequences. In his advice to her he urged gentleness toward self and others as the best way of driving out hardness and lack of charity. Only within the context of God's love should she "make war" on specific sinful dispositions. Under his regime of gentleness and balance the vehemence and harshness of the previous years began to abate. In mid-1934 she wrote, "My way should be that of dependence and abandonment. No more struggle to be what I think I'd like to be but a total yielding myself to God."[6]

Underhill's deep concern for the spiritual health of the church comes out in a letter that she wrote to the Archbishop of Canterbury before the 1930 Lambeth Conference urging the assembled bishops to call the clergy to a life of prayer. Her words speak of the need for good spiritual directors and, in her description of the needs of a priest, outlines the grounding that is essential to anyone working in spiritual direction:

All who do personal religious work know that the real hunger among the laity is not for halting attempts to reconcile theology and physical science but for the deep things of the spirit.

We look to the church to give us an experience of God, Mystery, Holiness, Prayer, which shall lift us to contact with the supernatural world—minister Eternal Life. We look to the clergy to help and direct our spiritual growth. We are seldom satisfied, because with a few noble exceptions they are so lacking in spiritual realism, so ignorant of the laws and experiences of the life of prayer. Their dealings with souls are often vague and amateurish. Those needing spiritual help may find much kindliness, but seldom that firm touch and first hand knowledge of interior ways that come only from a disciplined personal life of prayer.

God is the interesting thing about religion; and people are hungry for God. But only a priest whose life is soaked in prayer, sacrifice and love, can by his own spirit of adoring worship help us to apprehend Him. His secret correspondence with God—however difficult and apparently unrewarding—is the first duty of every priest. Divine renewal can only come through those whose roots are in the world of prayer: and therefore the two things the laity wants from the priesthood are spiritual realism and a genuine love of souls.[7]

In this call to personal holiness, Evelyn Underhill goes straight to the heart of prayer and asks for "realistic contact with the supernatural." In the accounts we have of her as a director we find the same. Deep listening helped her to enable people to be aware of the realities of their own lives as places for meeting God. Her grounded, incarnational, and sacramental approach encouraged people away from the dangers of over-spiritualizing or slipping into a simple and practical humanism.

Underhill's first retreat, given at Pleshey in 1924, was on her favorite topic of sanctity. In the opening address she speaks of silence:

Our deepest contacts with God are so gentle because they are all we can bear. We need quiet to experience them. They do not come as an earthquake of mental up-heaval or in the scorching fire or rushing wind of emo-tion. In the silence there is nothing devastating or sensational, but only a still small voice.

The titles she gave to her talks indicate her thinking on sanctity: Love, Joy, Peace, Prayer, The Communion of Saints, Growth, and Service. She works from passages in the Bible, from classic writers on the spiritual life, St. Augustine, Thomas à Kempis, St. John of the Cross, Julian of Norwich, and St. Ignatius among them, and from every-day human experience. A few quotations from the ad-dresses help give the flavor of her insight and directness:

> This peace, which St. Paul says must crown our love and our joy if they are genuine, is not merely a nice re-ligious feeling that comes to us in times of prayer. It does not mean basking in the divine sunshine like com-fortable pussycats. It means such a profound giving of ourselves to God, such an utter neglect of our own opin-ions, preferences and rights keeps the deeps of our souls within his atmosphere in all the surface rush, the ups and downs, demands and disappointments, joy and suffering of daily life. We cease to matter. Only God and His work matters.

> The connection between real holiness and homeliness is a very close one. Sanctity comes right down to and through all the simplicities of human life.[8]

All her core themes re-emerge throughout the retreats: searching for and openness to the reality of God, the indi-vidual's response in abandonment to God's will, the cen-trality of prayer, and the call to live out one's religion in the practical ways of relationships, attitudes, and activities.

Father Andrew, SDC

Roughly contemporary with Evelyn Underhill, Father Andrew (born Henry Ernest Hardy) was one of the founding members of the Society of Divine Compassion, a Franciscan religious community for men with a deep commitment to serve the poor. A large part of his ministry was spent at Plaistow in the East End of London, where the community was based in the parish of St.Philip's. The stories of his loving care for people there and his deep concern for their well-being are legendary. His importance for this book lies in his gifts as a director of souls, a retreat conductor, and a writer on prayer. In a letter to a friend written in 1900, he outlined his firm Anglican convictions:

> I find "X" such a kindred spirit, because the very illogical position of holding extreme Catholic views about the Sacraments and very broad Evangelical views about the love of God, and loving to live the life of a Friar, is the only position in which I have ever found rest. Whenever I have tried for the love of you to be less "high" or for the love of others to be less "low," I have always lost the content of soul that is, I believe, a real symptom that one is abiding in Christ.[9]

Although much in demand as a retreat conductor and spiritual director, Father Andrew did not like to spend too much time away from his parish and, like Underhill, carried on some of the work of spiritual direction through correspondence. We can get an insight into his way as a director from a letter written toward the end of his life to one of his directees:

> I have been praying for you and feel constrained to write to you about the matter of which you wrote to me. You know how loath I am ever to crush, and how I

would always seek to consecrate and to free, never to cripple and confine. At the same time it is our souls that have the right to the highest freedom. We are souls. Christian mortification does not set out to put fetters on the flesh; it sets out to knock the fetters off the spirit.

To another he wrote in 1939:

I will gratefully do my best to help you to live in union with the will of God for you.

If a person has a moderate ear for music they can detect if a piano is very much out of tune, but if it is moderately out of tune it will not distress them, because their ear is not sufficiently sensitive to detect the discord.

If a soul is spiritually underdeveloped, such a soul will feel unhappy if she falls into some great act of selfishness, but otherwise will not be troubled. As a soul attains to spiritual sensitiveness, so she becomes aware of any taint of self-centredness and self-will that mars the freedom of her service; she knows when she is out of tune.

We cannot go beyond our light or run ahead of our spiritual experience, but we must be loyal to the light we are able to see. The more we respond to the vision and the pressure of the will of God, the more sensitive will our souls become; and also the judgement on neglect and disobedience will always be a deadening of our sense of sin and appreciation of holiness.

Some people are helped by having a rule, but I think most serious people, though they may never write down a rule or consider that they keep one, do really live by rule. What I feel about a rule myself is that one wants to be very clear that it is a rule, something below which one will not let oneself drop; it is not an ideal, something to which one is trying to soar.

As a matter of fact all education is on much the same lines: (1) you find someone who can paint; (2) you watch that person painting; (3) you go away and try to paint yourself; (4) you bring back what you have done to the Master for criticism and correction; (5) you try again.

So a student learns to paint. Substitute for "student" the word "disciple" and for "someone who can paint" "the Incarnate Christ" and for "learning to paint" all that we mean by religion—learning to live, to love, to suffer, to succeed, to fail, to worship, to die—and your spiritual education will follow the lines of all education.

Gilbert Shaw and Mother Mary Clare

Born in 1886, Gilbert Shaw was an unusual man with unusual gifts. Although the institutional church failed to find a place for him, his life and ministry witness to his extraordinary insight and his passionate commitment. He came from a family of lawyers and began a career as a barrister before being ordained to a Berkshire curacy. His reading of St. John of the Cross and the guidance of Father William of Glasshampton led him on the way of Carmelite spirituality. He was for some time the secretary of the Association for Promoting Retreats before his years in parish ministry in the East End of London. There, as a committed Christian Socialist, he gave selfless service among the unemployed, seeking to put into practical effect his theology of the kingdom of God.

Shaw was much in demand as a spiritual director, with a great number of penitents seeking his help. He was psychically sensitive with a vivid awareness of the paranormal and of the occult and the world of spiritual conflict. Himself a rigorous ascetic, he taught the cost of a life of prayer. His *Pilgrim's Book of Prayers* was published in 1945, but he left no written teaching about the ministry of spiritual direction beyond the occasional letter:

> There is only one director and that is the Holy Spirit. I'm a pilgrim sitting at the roadside on the way to Jerusalem and as other pilgrims pass by I like to be able to give them a little word of encouragement to put them en route again.[10]

With his three great interests—the occult and the Christian's conflict with evil; his intense, active social concern; and his deep sense of spiritual affinity with St. John of the Cross—Shaw had a prophetic quality in his ability to read the signs of the times. It came to the fore in his lasting gift to the church, the fruit of the last ten years before he died, spent working closely with an Anglican religious order in Oxford, the Sisters of the Love of God, and in particular with the superior, Mother Mary Clare. This community was founded in 1906 by the Society of St. John the Evangelist, also known as the Cowley Fathers. It has a modern rule based on monastic principles and Carmelite spirituality, with the contemplative life as its main focus. Until Shaw's appointment, first as confessor and then as warden, the sisters had been under the guidance of the Cowley Fathers. Shaw helped to develop the community's life and renew its constitution. Drawing from sources in the church of the West and the Orthodox East, he centered his teaching on "the one great tradition" of contemplative life. He gave a new sense of the vital connection between the contemplative life and the life of society not only to this community, but also the monastery at Crawley Down in Sussex, where he was instrumental in the founding of the

Community of the Servants of the Will of God for men living the contemplative life.

Mother Mary Clare was superior of the Sisters of the Love of God for twenty years, from 1954, to 1973. She was a woman of deep contemplative prayer and notable strength of character, who shared with Gilbert Shaw the vision for renewing the community's life. Together their prophetic awareness brought a fresh direction and impetus to the sisters. Following her retirement as superior and until her death in 1988, she exercised a wide ministry as a director, especially among the clergy. Kenneth Leech has written of her:

Mary Clare was a powerful resource as the Church of England sought, with some uncertainty and puzzlement, to recover its ministry of spiritual direction. In July 1974 Sydney Evans, then dean of King's College, London, called together a small group to consider the future shape of this ministry with particular attention to the training of priests and pastors. Among those present were David Jenkins, later Bishop of Durham, Canon Evan Pilkington and Canon Adrian Somerset Ward (both of them experienced spiritual guides) and Mother Mary Clare.

Her paper, which was never published, was prophetic and wise. She emphasized four needs for the contemporary Church. First, the ability to "live with eternity," calling for deep inner resources of wisdom, spiritual discernment and vision. Second, the gift to know and interpret what God is doing in the present crisis of the world, and in the dying and rising of the Christian Church. She spoke of this as a "corporate dark night." Third, the commitment to the healing and wholeness of the human person and the human community, a commitment that was at the same time personal and social. Finally, the recognition of the role of the praying community as the spearhead of the conflict with the powers of darkness.[11]

Both Gilbert Shaw and Mother Mary Clare can be seen as people who were ahead of their time. Their awareness of the needs of society and its relationship with the contemplative life and also their recognition of collapse within the church have a clear message for today.

Reginald Somerset Ward

Largely because of his own insistence on the hidden and private nature of the ministry of spiritual counsel, Somerset Ward's gift to the church is not widely known. Yet in any account of the Anglican tradition of spiritual direction his work must feature as one of the most important influences of the twentieth century. In a lecture marking the thirtieth anniversary of Reginald Somerset Ward's death, Canon John Townroe remembered his first meeting with him in the side chapel of All Saints' Church, Newcastle-upon-Tyne:

> He was sitting well wrapped up, an overcoat underneath his surplice. There was no heating in the church. It was winter. His expression was serious but kindly and welcoming. He was sturdily built and gave an impression of strength. His face in repose could look stern, and so it could sometimes in action. But it would change in a flash to a twinkling, often puckish smile. Humour, gravity, lightness of touch, firmness—these qualities appeared and re-appeared as the occasion drew them out. As I remember him he struck me not as a judge ready to find fault, but more like a family doctor con-

cerned to make you well, concerned for release from any kind of sickness, concerned for wholeness.[12]

This was the man who for nearly fifty years gave himself to the full-time ministry of spiritual counsel. He worked as a curate in parishes in London, spent four years as secretary of the Church of England Sunday School Institute, and for two years served as rector of Chiddingfold in Surrey. His grandson describes how he then came to his life's vocation:

> He became certain that his calling was not to be a pastor in the normal sense, but to be a director of souls. He wrote to his bishop, Bishop Edward Talbot of Winchester, to explain. Talbot was sympathetic, but pointed out that the Church of England had no such position. Nevertheless, with a wife and two children, with no savings and no private resources at all, he resigned his living in the absolute faith that if he was doing the right thing—and he knew that he was—God would provide. And God did. For the remaining forty-seven years of his life he never held another paid job.[13]

At his home, "Ravenscroft" in Farncombe, and at one time in twenty centers across England, he was available to many hundreds of people. The demands that his peripatetic ministry made upon him were high. Traveling from center to center by train, he would see up to twelve people a day for half an hour each. Experienced directors today may marvel at the short time given to each person, but he had the gift of discerning what people needed and an ability to recognize the one key point to be worked on. He also pioneered what is now taken for granted, that the director and the individual sit together on two chairs. Within the allotted half hour, Ward's usual pattern was for the first part to be devoted to conversation and then perhaps a formal confession or the giving of a blessing. One of his directees wrote to me in a letter,

> An encounter with Somerset Ward could be an alarming experience. He had a commanding presence and most penetrating eyes—which although normally kindly or humorous, might at times become extremely stern! When someone came to see him, he would always sit the individual down for a period of frank discussion—"How are things going?"—"Any sense of reality in your prayers?"—leading on to particular problems or guidance about ways ahead. The confession, if it was to be heard, came right at the end of the proceedings.

When hearing confessions he was a great believer in the remedial penance. It was always regarded a form of thanksgiving for absolution and would often help a penitent towards amendment or some way of setting right a wrong tendency. His ability to think up a relevant penance was amazing and would have consequences reaching far beyond the walls of the confessional.

My own memories from the time when he was my director echo these reminiscences. In particular I remember his eyes: they seemed to have more circles in them than most other people's and I used to think that the innermost one was the Eye of God. I still carry the memory of his belief in a personal rule of life. His principle was that people should agree to a rule of life that was uncomplicated and definite; not a series of hopes but a firm pattern for spiritual life. A rule was for him something like an Old Testament sacrifice.

It had to be a worthy offering and once made it was meant to be kept.

> Your main duty in this world is to get the best out of your body, mind, and soul with which God has endowed you. You endanger this duty whenever you give up the right priorities that govern the spiritual life. The first priority is prayer, by which the soul has contact with God, and receives the life which alone gives lasting value to all that is done in this life. The second priority is rest and recreation without which the body cannot be kept fit for God's service ....The third priority is the work He gives you to do for His glory and purpose....If you get these priorities out of their right order, God loses (and incidentally, you suffer). In different lives, these priorities have different measures of time, but never of order.[14]

Rules were few and simple. More often than not they were to be expressed in terms of time, the one currency available to all. With his recognition of the importance of a rule to cover rest and relaxation, it is to Somerset Ward that we owe the insistence on the clergy taking a day off. I remember his injunction that if you do not let God do his work of refreshing you, how can you hope to do his work of ministry? He was also a believer in creative hobbies and himself worked in wood, making a doll's house and the carved panels of the altar in his own chapel.

Among his gifts to the souls he directed was Somerset Ward's skill in diagnosis. In the area of prayer and temperament, he recognized, there were three types of people.

> Friedrich von Hügel detected in all religion and in all prayer three elements: the Institutional, the external, authoritative, historical, traditional element and func-

tion of religion, which he found most strongly empha-
sised in the teaching of St. Peter; the Intellectual, the
reasoning, argumentative, abstractive element and
function, which he found set forth most clearly in the
teaching of St. Paul; and the Mystical, the experimental,
volitional, conscious, internal element, which he found
best expressed in the writings of St. John.... It will be
found by experience that in each human being who
strives in prayer one of the three elements is stronger
than the other two, and there is a greater inclination to
develop it.[15]

From his own work with the thousands of people who
came to him, he reckoned that between sixty and seventy
percent were ordinary churchgoers for whom the institutional aspect of Christianity was strongest. Some ten percent could be seen as following the path of the intellect to
God, while between twenty and twenty-five percent followed a mystical way. He had the God-given ability to discern people who had a mystical inclination and was deeply
concerned that they should be carefully directed, recognizing that not many had the ability to help them.

A letter that Somerset Ward wrote in 1930 to Edmund
Morgan, the future Bishop of Truro, shows how he himself
regarded the work of spiritual direction. Morgan was at the
time looking for a director and seeking advice on a possible
change of work. Somerset Ward wrote in reply:

I think I shall assist you best by simply telling you the
view I have reached concerning "spiritual direction" after twenty years experience of the work. I am struck in
the first place by the great dangers inherent in the work.
Chief among them I should place the risk of regarding
one's own opinion as inspired, the risk of stamping

one's own personality on persons of weak character, the risk of substituting psychology for Christianity.

Against these dangers we must place some undoubted advantages; it is as far as I can see almost impossible to get a clear view of one's own sins or weak spots without outside aid; experience counts for more in prayer than in any other art and can save much time and many disastrous mistakes; most people need at times in life the encouragement and support of someone whose advice they trust.

I should not be sincere if I did not confess that above and beyond these dangers and advantages there stands in my mind the experience I share with many other priests, an experience so constant and so proved that I cannot doubt it. It is the experience of being enabled, quite without my own volition, to see the need of a penitent or the exact knot at the centre of their difficulties. This experience leads me to believe that in spite of the worthlessness of the instrument God does use spiritual direction to help men and women to find and to follow Him.[16]

In the same letter, Ward's comments on the considerations to be borne in mind in choosing a director give a clear idea of the kind of contract that he believed spiritual direction involved:

As regards your seeking my help, I am quite clear. On my side there is no question. It is the work God has given me to do, and I must serve those who seek my help.

On your side, there is only one consideration. Do you sincerely believe God is calling you to seek direction and mine in particular? If you do, then use it. If you do not, on no account have anything to do with it.

Personally I have always liked you and respected you, but that is a minor point compared to what God wants us to do.[17]

Most of the books Somerset Ward wrote were published anonymously, as by either "A Priest" or "The Author of The Way." His three works on the spiritual life, *The Way*, *Following the Way*, and *To Jerusalem*, were made up of selections from the "instructions" that he sent out each month to those he directed, while others came from retreats and courses of instruction, like his *Guide for Spiritual Directors*. It is typical of the way Somerset Ward worked that, although he wrote these regular monthly instructions for his penitents, he did not write a major treatise on the work of spiritual direction. His *Guide*, though it contains his ideas, is of less importance than actual encounters with the man himself. Much of his written work is dated, moreover, and he tended to use a style that is hard to read today, but there is one book that should last as an important text in the corpus of Anglican mystical writing. It is his *The Road to the Mystical City of Jerusalem*, which was printed, for private circulation only, in 1918.

There is no doubt that someone's prayer and relationship with God was the main work of any meeting with him. The whole of life was important; work, rest, and recreation were part of the conversation. But at the heart was prayer and how to help remove the hindrances to openness with God. Ward wrote of his guide:

This book is a summary of the experience gained in forty years which have been given up entirely to the work of spiritual direction and the hearing of confessions, a work which has of necessity compelled the study of the inner thoughts and lives of many hundreds of human beings. It is offered not as an authoritative work but simply as a contribution of experience which may assist others to reach more final conclusions.

The starting point of this study of the work of dealing with the spiritual health or sickness of the individual must be to ascertain the nature, character and limitations of our task as priests of the Church of England. Our portion of the Catholic Church has always set forth a special conception of this work, differing from that of other Communions in its emphasis on some aspects of it. It is a conception set forth in its only authoritative form in the Prayer Book.

It would seem the task of the Spiritual Director in the Church of England is not that he should be a judge or a dictator issuing commands, but that he should be a physician of the soul whose main work is to diagnose the ills of the soul and the hindrances to its contact with God; and to find, as far as he is given grace, a cure for them.

He goes on to quote from Bishop Jeremy Taylor in words that describe his own ministry:

God hath appointed spiritual persons as guides for souls, whose office is to direct and to comfort, to give peace and to conduct, to refresh the weary and to strengthen the weak; and therefore to use their advice is that proper remedy which God hath appointed.[18]

Until recently a very significant aspect of Somerset Ward's ministry remained totally hidden from public view. The source of his great gifts as a spiritual director lay in the grace of mystical prayer that had been given to him in the early years of his priesthood, in which a vivid and direct experience of "The Lord Beloved" gave him a remarkable insight in his dealings with the people who came to him. From the accounts in his papers in Lambeth Palace Library, it is clear that a series of different spiritual events took place over about eleven years, beginning in 1911. In September of that year he was led to ask "the Beloved" to be his director, to whom Somerset Ward gave his absolute submission, and received "from Him my Rule of Life and Detachment." His grandson Richard Somerset Ward comments that these experiences

> took place not in a monastery or a hermitage, but while he was in the world, living his days in a torrent of activity and activism for the Sunday School Institute, as a priest, a husband and a father. If he was a mystic (and, yes, he was), and if he taught the Mystical Way to Christ (and, yes, he did), then he lived and taught these things in an entirely practical way. He speaks to me through his writings, just as he once spoke to me in the flesh, as an entirely practical guide to a life in, and of, the world, but a life that is dedicated solely to Christ.[19]

Somerset Ward recorded a number of intimate encounters "with the Lord Beloved in the Hidden Sanctuary." In 1914, at the offering of the Holy Sacrifice, he writes of being shown his self "like a mass of clinker with a spark of fire inside." The clinker was "diseased flesh" and the tiny spark "my soul....I have never known before the horror of sin, the sight brought on such nausea that it remained with me all day."[20]

Reading the vivid descriptions in the accounts of these showings, I have to admit to some sense of unease. The language is flowery and the images are intense and emotional.

Clearly the writer was struggling to put into words experiences that went beyond the capacity of ordinary language, often emphasizing that what he describes is not physical but "in the Holy Spirit." Two things reassure me. The first is that so often as he describes his meeting with his Lord there is a practical decision to be made as result, more often than not in the area of increased detachment. The second is the evidence provided by his ministry over the following fifty years in which he was so clearly used by God and the work of spiritual counsel rooted in his own relationship with his Lord.

"The Road to Jerusalem"

Training in the art of mystical prayer was the heart of Somerset Ward's teaching, yet as one contemporary wrote:

> He was not all in favor of opening up this teaching to "all and sundry," and in all my contacts with him over twenty five years he gave me clear instructions that what he called "The Road" should be secret.[21]

He used the metaphor of "the road" in two connected ways. In the broadest sense it simply meant the mystical way of prayer, but it was also the name of a fellowship that he formed of people who were called to follow that way. Somerset Ward was aware of the danger not only of spiritual pride among those called to the mystical way, but also of cheapening the gift of mysticism at a time when people were seeking ecstatic experience for all kinds of reasons. *The Road to the Mystical City of Jerusalem* was intended only for private circulation. In its story of a soul on the journey to Jerusalem, the work drew on the English pastoral tradition of the fourteenth-century mystics. The book's strength lies in the fact that it is clearly within the mainstream of Christian mystical writing; its weakness lies in its ornate style, coming from an era when the natural language for prayer in the Church of England was that of the *Book of Common Prayer*. Although he does not use the language of the sixteenth and seventeenth century, Ward's style of writing is mannered and seems artificial to the modern reader.

The book opens with what its author calls "the apology":

> In the chapel of Wolvesey Palace at Winchester He showed me a little light, like a jet, so exceeding hot that in a widening circle, that increased every moment, everything was melted; and it was an exceeding little light.
>
> And as I kneeled, with my head on His knees, I said, "Why is it so little, dear Lord?" And He said, "Because it dwelleth in thee."[22]

In six chapters this treatise follows the road from the camp to the city, using imagery from the letter to the Hebrews, "Let us therefore go forth unto Jesus without the camp, bearing his reproach. For we have not here an abiding city, but we seek after the city that is to come." The journey begins in the world known to us by our bodily senses:

> Standing then at the door of the tent the soul looks out towards the dawn. By this looking all is changed and made new. The new light shows more distinctly the Road that starts from the camp and loses itself in the morning mists, the little tracts that run in apparently meaningless tangle through the camp are seen to have their purpose in leading to the entering in of the Road and something of the charm of the wider horizon, the unlimited distance, is made plain.

The soul having turned its back for the moment on the camp of created things and the tent of Self, and having looked towards God, hears the words, "Let us go forth."

This response to the call leads to confusion and uncertainty on the soul's part. The traveler may seek the sacrament of confession or the guidance and counsel of a spiritual director, which is itself a sign of a determination to leave self-will behind.

In entering the road, the soul enters into the peace of God and the first stage of detachment, which is expressed in a rule of life. The traveler is urged to "begin with a little Rule and grow to a greater one." At this stage,

the detached soul is greatly occupied with prayer. Now there are three kinds of prayer. The first is vocal prayer. The second sort of prayer is mental prayer; and this is much more suited to the needs of the soul. By means of its thoughts it can convey to God in a short time what it would need hours to convey if the thoughts had to be expressed in words. The third sort of prayer is the prayer of the Hidden Sanctuary, where neither words nor thoughts are used, but only will and desire; and this is the prayer most suited to the needs of the soul on this Road, but it is only possible at times, and so the soul must always use mental prayer as well.

Ward also speaks of the many twists and turns that the traveler meets on the road to Jerusalem:

It is of the nature of a road that is should be perpetually changing. The soul is for ever passing on into new experiences and new purgings. The work of the Road is to purify the soul of Self in the senses, the will and the inmost life, and this can only be done by repeated purgings. These changes destroy the certainty of the soul and teach it how entirely it depends on God for all things.

It is because of the uncertain nature of the road that the soul needs the help of a guide. In a section of particular relevance to a book on spiritual direction, Ward writes:

> In choosing a Director the soul must consider, first his life, next his experience and thirdly the Divine Guidance. No Director can help the soul who is not manifestly following the Road himself, and if he is not detached, and is not marked by the Love of God, the soul is better without him. Nor can a Director help a soul unless he has experience, for he must know the stages of the Road, and the way to the Hidden Sanctuary, and the reality of the Presence before he can help any soul upon this Road. And lastly the soul has to consider whether God has put this Director in its way, and seems to will it to accept him as such, for if the direction be not by the will of God it will not help the soul. Also the Director should be very humble, that he may become an empty shell for God to work through.
>
> I pray the Lord of the Road to raise up some worthy Directors for the use of souls on this Road, for He knows what great need there is of them.

Because he knew that the mystical way of prayer was understood by only a few, Ward taught it only to those who really desired this teaching for themselves. Before joining the "fellowship of the road," they had to answer four questions and agree to four safeguards. The questions focused on the central importance of the call to mystical prayer:

Do you voluntarily and of your own free will choose to follow this Road to God?

Are you prepared to give up all you possess, all that you desire and all that you hope for in order to come to God?

Are you willing to undergo suffering, humiliation, mortification and the crucifixion of the soul?

Do you accept the test of the Road by giving your obedience to your Director on the Road subject to the safeguards appointed for that purpose?

These safeguards ensured that each soul retained his or her own responsibility for choice:

At any moment and without giving any reason the soul can withdraw its obedience on its sole responsibility.

Anything commanded under obedience that is clearly against the Commandments or the Sermon on the Mount is null and void.

Any previous vow, promise or obligation that is not clearly against God's laws remains unaltered by the obedience.

A reason can in every case be demanded for anything ordered under obedience, though the reason may not be pleasing or satisfying to the soul.

The first person to "enter the road" was Somerset Ward's colleague at the Sunday School Institute, Phyllis Dent. From 1911 until his death in 1962, he admitted 225 people to the fellowship, which continued to grow after his death under Ward's successor, Norman Goodacre. Some of those joining the fellowship were Anglican priests, but women—including many deaconesses—formed the vast majority. Each person was asked to pray daily for the next entrant and to continue praying when that person passed over "the little wall of death" into the life beyond.

The hiddenness that formerly marked this ministry has given way to an open acceptance of the need for spiritual counsel, and there are many directors today who owe much at first, second, or even third hand to the gifts that God gave to the Church of England through this gifted spiritual director and teacher. Eric Abbott, dean of Westminster Abbey, spoke for all at Somerset Ward's memorial service:

> We thank God openly for a priest whose ministry was hidden, for the special grace that was his as a director of souls, for the costly, patient obedience that he rendered to his God-given vocation through the years. For the active trust in God which he taught, to cast out fear, for the way in prayer which he helped us to follow, for the atoning love and power of Christ which he helped us receive in the ministry of absolution. For his deep and passionate love for the Church of England, for his cure of souls that was charismatic and, because charismatic, was wise with the wisdom of God, discerning with the piercing of the Spirit's sword, stern with the divine judgement, and compassionate with the Redeemer's mercy.[23]

Endnotes

1. W. R. Inge, *Christian Mysticism* (London: Methuen, 1899), 5.

2. Charles Williams, ed., *The Letters of Evelyn Underhill* (London: Darton Longman & Todd, 1989), 25.

3. Dana Greene, ed., *Evelyn Underhill: Modern Guide to the Ancient Quest for the Holy* (New York: State University of New York Press, 1988), 2.

4. Quoted in Joy Milos, "Evelyn Underhill: A Companion on Many Journeys" in *Traditions of Spiritual Guidance*, ed. Lavinia Byrne (London: Geoffrey Chapman, 1990), 138; 140; 131; 135.

5. Williams, *Letters*, 26.

6. Dana Greene, *Evelyn Underhill: Artist of the Infinite Life* (New York: Crossroad, 1991), 104.

7. From an unpublished manuscript.

8. Grace Aldolphsen Brame, ed., *The Ways of the Spirit* (New York: Crossroad, 1990), 51; 71; 99.

9. Quotations from the letters are drawn from Kathleen Burne, *The Life and Letters of Father Andrew, SDC* (London and Oxford: Mowbray, 1948), 90; 49; 215; 218.

10. R. D. Hacking, *Such a Long Journey: A Biography of Gilbert Shaw, Priest* (London: Mowbray, 1988), 38.

11. Kenneth Leech, "Encountering the Depths: The Spirituality of Mother Mary Clare SLG" in *Christian* 16 (1989).

12. John Townroe, Somerset Ward Memorial Lecture, Guildford Cathedral, October 3, 1992.

13. Richard Somerset Ward, *Fairacres Chronicle* 29:1: 34.

14. Ibid., 37.

15. Reginald Somerset Ward, *A Guide for Spiritual Directors* (London and Oxford: Mowbray, 1957), 47.

16. MS 3235 in Lambeth Palace Library.

17. *Ibid.*

18. Ward, *Guide*, 7.

19. Richard Somerset Ward, *Fairacres Chronicle* 29:1:36.

20. MS 3584 in Lambeth Palace Library.

21. MS 3548 in Lambeth Palace Library.

22. The following quotations are from Reginald Somerset Ward, *The Road to the Mystical City of Jerusalem* (privately printed, 1918), 15-56 *passim*.

23. Service paper, Westminster Abbey.

Chapter 6

The American Experience

The preceding chapters have shown how in England the tradition of spiritual direction existed continuously, if sometimes hidden from view, within the Anglican church from its earliest days. The story is very different in America where, as the twentieth century comes to an end, we find that spiritual direction stands out as a strong feature of life in its mainline churches. In the association known as Spiritual Directors International there is even the beginnings of what amounts to a professional body, with a membership approaching three thousand people—mostly Roman Catholics, but including two hundred Episcopalians. The main purpose of this chapter, therefore, is to look at the extraordinary revival of the ministry of spiritual direction and to see what part the Episcopal Church has played in it, to look at some of the people who have been involved, and to note some of its particular trends.

This widespread interest in spiritual direction on the part of the Episcopal Church is a comparatively recent phenomenon. When I looked for writings on spiritual guidance by Episcopalians, or collections of letters of direction written in the late nineteenth and early twentieth centuries of the kind that are plentiful in the Church of England, I was surprised to find virtually none at all. Certainly there is evidence of the practice of sacramental confession, which includes the giving of counsel and advice, in the Anglo-Catholic wing of the church. For instance, there has been a strong tradition among religious orders like the Society of St. John the Evangelist and the Order of the Holy Cross of the importance of this ministry. What I did find, on the other hand, was that in the years following the World War II Episcopalians were complaining about a recognized lack of spiritual formation among the clergy and calling for greater weight to be given to the practice of prayer in the preparation of the clergy for ministry, although spiritual direction receives little mention at this time. One contemporary observed:

> Evidence is growing that, among both clergy and laity, men are eager and hungry to learn more fully and deeply of the life of praying. More and more men are coming to acknowledge frankly their abysmal ignorance concerning the all-important relationship with God in prayer. Men instinctively look to the Church and to the clergy for help and for teaching in prayer. Where else may they look?

> The riches and depths of the life of Christian praying are commonly unknown. In the theological seminaries of most of the churches one must search long and far to find courses offering serious and systematic instruction in the spiritual life. Here again it is taken for granted that the theological student has somehow already acquired the knowledge, understanding, discipline and practice of truly Christian praying. Theological education has been and still is predominantly intellectual—the imparting of correct conceptions about God. The divinity schools are theological and intellectual in emphasis, rather than spiritual.[1]

Until the late 1970s, therefore, it was rare to hear talk of spiritual direction in America, and rarer still to find individuals who described themselves as spiritual directors.

The Order of Holy Cross

Among those who kept alive the tradition of spiritual guidance within the American religious orders, one name stands out in particular. Shirley Hughson, a monk of the Order of the Holy Cross, was superior of the order for several periods between the two world wars in alternation with Alan Whittemore. Their two strong personalities were strongly contrasted. Whittemore's deep faith and committed spirituality expressed itself in radical social concern, whereas Hughson was widely recognized as a holy man and was in much demand as a director of souls, particularly among religious communities on both sides of the Atlantic. Before his death in 1950 Hughson published a manual entitled *Spiritual Guidance*, which is a classical work of ascetic theology full of references to the patristic theologians, to the mystics, and to French spiritual writers of the seventeenth, eighteenth, and nineteenth centuries.

It is fascinating to see how in many of the letters of direction that he wrote, collected, and published after his death, there is this same reliance on classical tradition with little or no sign that contemporary psychology had anything helpful to say about people's problems. Only twenty years separate these books of his, which are in effect works from the past, from the writings of the 1970s and 1980s with their widely different approach to the subject. As an example of his style and approach, notice how he writes on the ministry of spiritual direction as

> the systematic guidance of souls in such a course of interior activities, as will remove obstacles to the activities

of God within us, and issue in the spiritualizing and divinizing of the whole life.... The aim of spiritual direction is so to educate the soul that, realizing spiritual values, and ready always to respond to them, it will be conscious of the continual and progressive call of the Holy Spirit and know how to follow the call in such a manner that its perfection will be ever on the increase and God be the more glorified and honored in it.

To direct the soul is to lead it in the ways of God; it is to teach the soul to listen for the divine inspiration and to respond to it; it is to suggest to the soul the practice of all the virtues proper for its particular station; it is not only to preserve the soul in purity and innocence, but to advance it to perfection. In a word, it is to contribute as much as possible to the raising of the soul to the degree of sanctity which God has destined for it. It is thus that St. Gregory thought of direction when he said that the guidance of souls is "of all arts, the most excellent."[2]

The historian of the Order of the Holy Cross, Adam Dunbar McCoy, mentions Hughson's striking lack of modern psychological insight. *The Warfare of the Soul*, published in 1910, he wrote,

is completely unaffected by contemporary psychology and posits a theory of personality which differs little from classical and medieval *psychomachias*.... The Christian life is fundamentally a personal, not a social or communal, matter.[3]

This characteristic of his pastoral approach is well shown in a letter that Hughson wrote in 1912 to "A spiritual daughter who later became a religious":

I was giving our Sisters an instruction a few nights ago, when it came to me how that the spiritual warfare is not a struggle merely against temptation as we commonly think of it, but that every act of devotion is a definite attack on Satan, and that he is weaker in his warfare against all men for every blow that we smite him in the power of the Cross. It is a very comforting thought that by our prayer, well prayed, we are able to help every tempted soul in the world. Satan plans to assault some soul tomorrow, but we in the interim have prayed well, we have said an office with recollection, or made a meditation with resolute attention; and in consequence of this, when the time comes for the assault, he finds himself crippled because in that exercise well performed we struck him with the sharpness of the Cross.

In this work of spiritual warfare, Hughson was totally convinced of the centrality of prayer:

We Americans need more than anything else to pray to God to teach us to pray. If we really believe in prayer, and if we think it has power why do we not do more of it? It is a significant thing that these cloistered communities—there are quite a number of them in the English Church—are being blessed with increase, their novitiates are large, and the number of aspirants are increasing continually.... They seem to have a sense of spiritual repose, which is so necessary for deep prayer. Would that we could do something more of this kind in our country.

As to contemplation, I have been for a long time convinced that this is the thing that souls need. If we had more of it in the Church, the Church would be stronger and holier. I have been doing some work along these lines of late, and I should like, if I had the ability, to write a book on the subject. It needs explication. These days men are running after so-called efficiency, not knowing that the highest efficiency can only come from keeping open the channels which connect the soul directly with God. It is the wisdom and the strength of God that really enables, and that is not to be had through external organization. This poor old American Church of ours has tried efficiency with the result that it is practically bankrupt. If they prayed more, not in their prayers asking God for things either, but just loving and praising Him, a new strength would be infused into the whole life of the Church which would mean rejuvenation, and a going forth to great conquests for God.

He was well aware of the wider church beyond the religious orders, and the need for the ministry of prayer to be extended to the parish churches and their lay people:

I wish that in all our parishes there could be a real understanding of the fact that dogma is only the basis. A man may lay the foundations of a house and then build nothing on it. Our Christian life is after all a loving, personal and intimate relation of friendship with our Lord. It is distressing to see, as one not infrequently does, a group well grounded in the facts of the faith, but which has not been taught that it was the foundation for a life lived in Christ, a warm, loving union with Him that permeates life in its every department.

We get a small insight into Hughson's approach to spiritual direction in an excerpt from a letter he wrote to a young woman who later joined a religious order:

I have no claim to infallibility of judgement, but I have no hesitation in counselling you about your position. Resign by all means. As I say, this would free you for whatever action God might call you to. The more the matter simmers in my mind (and I always find that this simmering brings the best and most mature judgement), the more certain do I feel that God wants you for Himself.

In addition to his prodigious correspondence, Hughson was a supreme teller of stories. This description of his experience on vacation in Interlaken is one of very few personal stories in all the letters in the collection:

> Last evening I had my supper on the hotel terrace, the stupendously vast bulk of the Jungfrau stood up in front of me, 13,000 feet against the blue evening sky. The sun had gone behind the lesser mountains, but was still bathing in its full glory the upper slopes of the great peak, converting it into an immense crystal of purest gold. I sat watching it for nearly two hours, *contemplating* it. I did not use my intellect to study it. The thought of its height hardly suggested itself; it did not occur to me to consider the sharpness of its peaks or the depth of those drifts that have lain unmelted for thousands of years. I can think now of a thousand wonderful things about it, but they did not occur to me last night. I simply sat and drank in all its beauty. My mind was quiescent, so to speak, but down in my soul there were activities at work carving impressions upon my inner self that will never be effaced.

> Now put God in the place of the great work of His Hands, and let the same process go on. There you have contemplation.[4]

The Cowley Fathers in America

Another important thread in the Episcopal story begins in what was then a village on the outskirts of Oxford, England where Richard Meux Benson became vicar of the parish church of Cowley in 1850. Raised in a strongly evangelical family, as an undergraduate he came under the influence of Pusey and the Oxford Movement. Benson experienced a strong desire to go as a missionary to India but was persuaded that his duty lay in serving his parish. In 1866 he founded what later became the Society of St. John the Evangelist, the first Anglican religious community for men to survive and take its lasting place in the life of the church. Two other priests joined him in the beginning: one also from an evangelical background, Simon Wilberforce O'Neill, the other a high-church Episcopalian, Charles Grafton. They took the name of the Mission Priests of St. John the Evangelist and were dedicated to working in their parish to the east of Oxford, as well as to giving retreats and leading parish missions in different parts of the country.

Benson was committed to a low-key approach and full integration in the life of the diocese of Oxford and the Church of England as a whole, and he rejected what were seen at the time as Anglo-Catholic excesses. In a letter he cautioned:

> We must be careful not to let ourselves be carried away by the desire of ritual. I think one feels that the highest type of worship for us on earth is that plainness which S. Bernard would have inculcated. We should always remember that ritual is not for the purpose of pleasing ourselves. It is the offering of wealth, in form, art and substance to God for His glory, since all creation belongs to Him.[5]

Under his leadership the community developed as an attempt to fuse the twin purposes of a monastic order and a society of mission priests. Benson's own writings and addresses show him to have been deeply contemplative, with a solid basis in his devotion to Scripture. He had extraordinary power as a retreat conductor. His teaching was firmly based on the Bible and the early church fathers, and he looked for the Holy Spirit to renew the lives of individuals:

> We should always read the Bible as God's own Word, speaking to ourselves. We must consider the circumstances under which the Word of God came to men of old, and we must take care to read it with a watchful observance of what distinguished those ancient characters one from another. We must see in what way we ourselves differ from them. We must seek Christ in every word, for Moses and the Psalms and the Prophets all spake of Him.[6]

> The Spirit speaking in our hearts gives power and efficacy to the voice of conscience. The Spirit makes the glory of Christ to shine within us. This Spirit makes the conscience to ring with the unutterable power of the Word of God.[7]

Above all it is the retreats that he gave to his own community during their annual retreats that stand out in all the accounts of his life and work. His own deep spirituality shone through the words of his addresses, in which the Incarnation was always a central theme:

> The vision which dazzles those that are at a distance is the strength of those that are most near. As thou comest on, come on with all the fullness of the Eagle's gaze. So it is that God calls us near unto Himself by the Person of His Incarnate Word, throned in the glory of the ever-

lasting light. He calls us near unto Himself. And we if we would worship Him must know Him thus truly as He is. Yes, dear Brothers, so should it be with us. Let us seek to realise the greatness of the worship we are able to pay, which we can only pay in and through Jesus Christ.[8]

The spiritual insight and excitement of the loving response to God's invitation that were part of his inspiration are well shown in Benson's advice on meditation, which in structure closely followed the pattern of the Ignatian spiritual exercises:

Constant aspirations and devout acknowledgements uttered throughout the time of meditation, in sweet *colloquy* with God, are the really important part of the meditations. Sometimes, perhaps, these find their strongest utterance in the profound silence with which the soul waits upon God. God hears when we are silent, if our silence is the silence of Love.

Meditation must not make us dreamy and unpractical, for then it could not be true. If by meditation we come to see more of the Life of God, our meditation will lead us to show forth in our lives more truly the Life of God.[9]

Introducing the volume of Benson's letters, the Bishop of Vermont, Arthur Hall, SSJE, writes of the power and the delicacy of his pastoral counsel:

As a spiritual director Father Benson truly exemplified the dictum that a priest should be as a lion in the pulpit but a lamb in the confessional. Severe of course he could be on occasion, and uncompromising with evil in any form he always was, but wonderfully patient and considerate, and careful not to overdrive the flock. Probably the awe with which every one regarded him, on account of his goodness and his greatness, and from the sense of a certain separateness, was least felt when seeking his ministry in confession, for then his tenderness would be specially manifest. The heart of fire towards God he truly had, and the heart of steel towards himself, but not less the heart of flesh towards his brethren.[10]

Something of these qualities are shown in a letter that Benson wrote to a woman who was concerned about the fact that she did not feel it right to accept his advice:

A director's counsel plainly is only *counsel*. You must make up your own mind in such a matter, and act according to the interior leanings of God's Holy Spirit. You need not therefore feel in any way hampered because your judgement is not the same as his. It is no disrespect to him, nor any violation of the relationship in which you stand to him. Direction does not involve monastic obedience.[11]

In the 1870s Benson traveled to America and founded a house of the community in Cambridge, Massachusetts, with Charles Grafton and Oliver Prescott as its first members. After his resignation as Superior General, Benson himself continued to live in America. Since then a separate American congregation of the Society of St. John the Evangelist has been created, and recent years have seen remarkable growth in the life of the community under the leadership of Paul Wessinger, Thomas Shaw, now Bishop of Massachusetts, and Martin Smith. The visitor gets a sense that the vision of the community's founder finds fulfillment in the mixture of monastic community life with an emphasis also on spiritual direction, retreats, and mission outreach both to parishes and through youth work in Boston's inner city.

The Sixties and Seventies

With the coming of the 1960s all of the American churches were hit by a succession of different forces. The effects of Vatican II were just beginning to be widely felt not only among Roman Catholics but in other denominations as well: the decisions taken by the council were a kind of permission for all Christians to think new thoughts and to live with different attitudes. It was also during the early sixties that the American Protestant churches became caught up in the human potential movement and the corresponding wave of psychological awareness and new therapies that swept the country. Therapy, or pastoral counseling, came to be regarded as an essential tool that pastors needed for their ministry. It was the time of the Vietnam war and the protest movement, with all that the conflict meant for the conscience of the nation and the witness of the churches. (As an Englishman it is not easy for me to identify with the continuing power of the Vietnam experience on the nation's self-awareness and on its spirituality, but the Battle of the Somme in the First World War raises the same sort of powerful echoes in me, and I was born ten years after the war was over.) Consequently, the notion of an orderly discipline of prayer and rule of life seemed irrelevant, even meaningless, swamped as the churches were by the many conflicts of the day in that era of radical individualism, self-discovery, and the awakening social consciousness that was brought by the civil rights movement.

Those same conflicts, however, also gave a renewed urgency to people's need for a sense of meaning and purpose; with time came a dawning recognition that the god of psychotherapy did not always meet that need. Towards the end of the 1970s a movement to recover some of the traditional spiritual disciplines as part of a quest for an authentic spirituality began to gather momentum within the churches. In a study of clergy and ministers to assess their attitudes to spirituality, theologian Terry Holmes found that the idea of spiritual direction met with mixed reactions, all the way from a warm welcome to a fear of intrusion and the danger of being manipulated. Holmes noted a longing for spiritual companionship, which was often obscured by the effects of a personal history of disappointment, and concluded that his own ministry in this area was

> to share in another's particular pilgrimage. That journey is of necessity an inner exploration, so I seek to help a person identify his or her internal experience and relate it to the Gospel and its explication in Christian tradition... and in doing this I expect that my friend will both find room to develop his or her own unique style and will discern a particular direction in which he or she is moving by God's intention.[12]

Several streams flowed together in the recovery of spiritual direction among Episcopalians. Together with the important liberating effect of Vatican II came the renewal—I think of it as a kind of neo-Ignatian revival—among Jesuits in North America. It provided a vigor and sense of humanity to what had become a rather dry, systematized, and "text-driven" spirituality. Jesuit centers that had a strong influence on this renewed spirituality were Guelph in Ontario and the Weston School of Theology, whose arrival on the Episcopal Divinity School campus in Cambridge, Massachusetts brought fresh insights to the training in spirituality and spiritual direction there. The Jesuits John English and John Veltri are known for their pioneering work in adapting the insights and method of Ignatius to the late twentieth century, while William A. Barry and William J. Connolly published one of the first contemporary basic texts for spiritual directors, *The Practice of Spiritual Direction.* Without a doubt, however, it was the publication of Kenneth Leech's *Soul Friend* that helped to open the flood gates for Anglicans, especially for Episcopalians. This hugely influential book gave to people who were aware of their own spiritual needs and the needs of others a new language for exploring them, as well as the excitement of discovering the immediate relevance of skills and disciplines that had previously seemed remote and specialized. American as well as British readers can echo the words of George Carey, Archbishop of Canterbury, in his foreword to the second edition:

> When it was first published, *Soul Friend* opened a door for me, and for many of my generation. It was a door through which we could walk and discover more of the richness of Christian spirituality. My predecessor, Michael Ramsey, was quite right when he said of it: "Here at last we have a work on the cure of souls which understands the trends of the present day and at the same time draws upon the deep tradition of Christian spirituality in the work of counsellor, confessor and spiritual director."[13]

Leech offered a way of accompanying people on their journey of faith that connected with his readers' experiences, a way of looking at spiritual direction that both religious professionals and lay people could see might work in their own situation. *Soul Friend* was published in 1974 and it was followed by an extraordinary number of books published in the United States, the majority by Roman Catholics but also a significant number of works by Episcopalians like Alan Jones, Tilden Edwards, Rachel Hosmer, Julia Gatta, Martin Smith, and Margaret Guenther. Tilden Edwards, an Episcopal priest, director of the ecumenical Shalem Institute, and one of the leading figures in the revival of spiritual direction, brings a wide understanding of the range of different spiritualities, Christian and non-Christian. The work of Shalem is marked by a special emphasis on the contemplative nature of spiritual direction. In his 1980 book *Spiritual Friend: Reclaiming the Gift of Spiritual Direction* Edwards gives a clear appraisal of the world in which direction takes place and a detailed account of the many streams that flow into its practice, from the scriptures of the Old and New Testament, through the experience of the early church—particularly the desert fathers and mothers—to contemporary gifts of psychotherapy.

The re-emergence today of spiritual companionship as an important resource for a wide spectrum of people reflects a number of current human needs emerging from recent history. The first is a need for personal help in the growing collapse of a shared world-view within the Church, and cultural support without, for a Christian "way of life." Everyone is on his own now to choose between the myriad, sometimes contradictory visible options the Church and Society offer for a way of life.

A second need calling for more weight on personal spiritual guidance today emerges from the sense of limitation in educational and professional therapeutic relationships. Psychologically aware spiritual direction is a potentially invaluable resource.

A third need calling out such guidance comes from the starved half of the social activist. In the sixties most social activists (except those rising out of the black Church) were deeply suspicious of any kind of interior focus beyond confession of social sin. The personal self was to be sacrificed to the social self. In the seventies there was a clear shift with many such people. Something proved inadequate and empty about a totally exteriorized and communalized life. Something more interior and uniquely attentive to their personal situation was called for. It was not therapy they sought. It was their soul.

Finally, spiritual direction is receiving special attention in the face of our reawakening to the neglect of a careful oral tradition of spiritual guidance in the Church. Today we are almost totally dependent on books and scholarship for reminding us of the depths and nuances of human interior development that have been known in the light and path of Christian experience. We have been largely missing the careful, chastened, long-term, faith-grounded, tested, and intuitive person-to-person conveyance of the heart of Christian awareness. Such a situation cries out for a spiritual friend who can be with us not only through crisis, but through the more mundane times of spiritual attentiveness in our lives.[14]

Other landmarks along the way of the development of spiritual direction among Episcopalians include the founding of the Center for Christian Spirituality at the General Theological Seminary in New York. Alan Jones, its first director, came newly from England to the faculty of General and was among the first to popularize spiritual direction among Episcopalians. He was largely responsible for initiating the center to foster the serious study of spirituality and spiritual direction through courses designed to lead to the awarding of academic degrees, a pattern to be seen in many other spirituality training courses. Alan Jones has written widely in the area of spirituality and other themes, beginning with *Journey Into Christ*. His *Exploring Spiritual Direction* deals at some length with the question of relating spiritual direction to counseling and therapy.

In 1974 he was joined by Rachel Hosmer, a remarkable woman who was part of the original group that founded the Order of St. Helena in 1945. In her long life (she died at eighty) she worked for several years in Liberia, had close connections with religious communities in France and Britain, and in 1974 went to the General Seminary in New York to study for a degree in preparation for ordination. There she worked closely with Alan Jones in the newly established center and exercised a wide ministry of spiritual direction. In her introduction to Hosmer's autobiography, theologian Patricia Wilson Kastner wrote of her:

> She was a religious and a priest; a common combination for males but most rare among women. She had been one of the founding members of her community, and had been a strong if sometimes controversial voice among Episcopal religious. In the seventies, she was the first ordained woman to be a full-time member of General's faculty. Faculty and students alike had told me much about her intelligence, compassion, fearsome conscience, concern for peace and justice issues, and her gentle but astonishing capacity to grasp the depths of another's character.[15]

Distinctive Characteristics

We have mentioned some of the people and places that have been important in the development of spiritual direction in America. What are some of the distinctive characteristics that the discipline has assumed the United States?

For one, there is the huge importance of the psychiatric research done in America, and I will discuss spiritual direction's relationship with therapy and counseling in a later chapter. I also recognize the importance of European writers and models, as well as those from American Roman Catholicism: writers such as Evelyn Underhill, Baron von Hügel, C. S. Lewis, Thomas Merton, Henri Nouwen, Thomas Keating, and John Maine appear regularly in footnotes and references in books on spiritual direction. I hear them quoted in countless addresses and conversations. But in the end I recognize that there is a certain tone that marks the American Anglican approach to spiritual direction that differs from both the British and Roman Catholic authors who are responsible for the bulk of the work on the subject.

Important characteristics of an American attitude to spiritual direction include a strong sense of its relationship to and dependence on personal experience, both individual and corporate. Sandra Schneiders, writing in 1984, described current studies on spiritual direction in terms of their intimate and frankly acknowledged dependence on the personal experience of the respective authors. She saw little attempt to situate the current revival of interest in spiritual direction in the context either of history or of biblical or systematic theology. One aspect of this valuing of personal experience is the widespread and deep reliance on the teachings and to some extent the values of different schools of psychology and psychotherapy.

The story of the development of spiritual direction in America also shows the influence of a number of movements for renewal or for pastoral care and healing that have a strong independent life of their own. Among them are Alcoholics Anonymous, Cursillo, and the charismatic revival. The undisputed success of AA as a method for helping people suffering from alcoholism has inspired the creation of a range of similar twelve-step programs concerned with other sorts of addictive behavior. AA began in the 1930s as the creation of Bill Wilson, known in the history of AA as "Bill W." and himself an alcoholic. He came under the influence of the Oxford Group, got sober, and worked out the original "six steps," which were similar to the personal discipline advocated by the Oxford Group. The foundation of Alcoholics Anonymous can be dated from the time when Bill W. recruited Dr. Bob Smith; his nurse, a religious sister, introduced them to a Jesuit friend who contributed to the development of the Twelve Steps. The result is an interesting marriage of Ignatius and Calvin.

The link between these programs of recovery and spiritual direction is twofold. A great many Christians in the United States acknowledge having either found or rediscovered faith through their journey out of some kind of addiction by means of a twelve step program. They have learned their own inability to find their healing and their need to rely on a power outside themselves. This learning has been in the company of others, as they work through the steps with the companionship of their own sponsor, someone who has personal experience of the process in their own life. The parallels between this form of sponsoring and spiritual direction are very close. The process invites people to be open and honest in a small group and to recognize their need for the help both of a higher power and also of other people.

Cursillo, a movement for personal Christian renewal, is also to be found in many Episcopal dioceses today. Reactions to it range from vigorous support and encouragement through a wary tolerance to mild hostility. Its roots lie in Spanish Catholicism and its strongly Latin character is often the cause of anxiety among Anglicans. At the heart of the process is a short, very concentrated retreat designed to give participants an experience of the love of God and the welcome of the community, leading to a deepening of their commitment. The rituals of Cursillo have been criticized for their elements of secrecy and manipulativeness, which are more likely to be avoided in those places where Cursillo has been most fully adapted to Anglican norms. The gifts that it brings to people are a firm Christian commitment, the opportunity for formal learning, and the support of a continuing small group.

What makes it relevant here is Cursillo's recommendation that everyone who has "made their Cursillo" should have a spiritual director. It is not clear what spiritual direction means for the movement and perhaps it indicates someone more like a prayer companion than the kind of spiritual director that most of this book describes. However, the frequency of Cursillo events and the number of people affected has without doubt helped to raise the profile of spiritual direction in the Episcopal Church, as well as in Roman Catholic and Protestant churches. In particular, there are a good number of Episcopal clergy who have turned to spiritual direction in response to the requests of people in their parishes who have been through Cursillo.

The charismatic movement does not emphasize spiritual direction as such. But among its many strengths is the greater openness that it fosters in the Christian community about things of the spirit. Faith and living the Christian life become natural things to talk about in charismatic churches, whereas in many Anglican congregations they are regarded still as personal, too private for polite conversation.

Women and Spiritual Direction

The large part that has been played by women in spiritual direction marks the greatest contrast between the tradition we explored in the early chapters of this book and the situation we have today. As we look at the past, there is no doubt that, with notable exceptions, the people who gave spiritual guidance and who wrote or taught about it were mostly ordained men. To judge by the evidence in the different collection of "spiritual letters," moreover, the majority of people who looked to these men for guidance were women. Today on both sides of the Atlantic the majority of the people who are undertaking training to develop their effectiveness in this ministry are women and a very large proportion of them are lay people.

The wider story of twentieth-century feminism with its achievements, passions, and conflicts lies outside the scope of this book. There are, however, aspects that have a clear bearing on the life and ministry of women within Anglicanism. The work of direction has been changed and is changing as a result of what the women's movement has brought to the church. Although there are in Britain important thinkers, writers, and campaigners in the development of the women's cause within the churches, it is from America that much of its impetus has come.

Although clearly there have been in all ages sensitive male spiritual guides for women, the patriarchal model of government, leadership, and responsibility within the church has meant that the images of Christian spirituality and Christian life-style have followed male rather than female models of belief and behavior. The church has tended to value the male interest while ignoring or undervaluing female experience and gifts. In past ages this was reinforced by teachings that saw male authority as God-given and that emphasized the subservient virtues for women: obedience, sacrifice of self for others, and self-denial. Change has come about with the secular movement for women's rights as human beings throughout the western world, as the movement has fought for equal pay, equal opportunities in work, and full political recognition. Within the church women's enfranchisement has come about through a growing awareness of the distinctive talents that women bring to all areas of ministry. The ordination of women as priests and bishops is an important but by no means unique aspect of this.

As part of this breakthrough towards giving full value to the actual experience of women in their everyday lives, psychologist Carol Gilligan's *In a Different Voice* shows that there is a consistency and truth in the female approach that is not echoed in the mainstream of psychological and ethical teaching based almost entirely on male values and male attitudes. This approach is well illustrated in priest and spiritual director Margaret Guenther's distillation of her experience and learning in a wise, attractively written book called *Holy Listening: The Art of Spiritual Direction*, which shows the work of God among us in ordinary human experience. Guenther takes the images of hospitality, teaching, and midwifery as representing important aspects of the ministry of direction. "What happens when we offer hospitality?" she asks.

> Most simply, we invite someone into our space, a space that offers safety and shelter. The host's needs are put aside, as everything is focused on the comfort and refreshment of the guest. For a little while, at least, *mi casa es tu casa*, as the Spanish gracefully puts it. There are provisions for cleansing, food and rest. It is an occasion for storytelling where both laughter and tears are acceptable. After an interval of hospitality the guest

moves on, perhaps with some provisions or a road map
for the next stage of the journey. At its simplest hospitality is a gift of space, both physical and spiritual. Like
the gift of attentive listening, it is not to be valued
lightly.

Guenther goes on to explore the roles of the spiritual director as both teacher and midwife.

So what does the spiritual director teach? In its simplest
and also most profound terms, the spiritual director is
simultaneously a learner and a teacher of discernment.
What is happening? Where is God in this person's life?
What is the story? Where does this person's story fit in
our common Christian story? How is the Holy Spirit at
work in this person's life? What is missing?

With the incarnation at the center of our faith, it is not
surprising that our language of piety is filled with the
imagery of birthgiving.... The midwife is present to another in a time of vulnerability, working in areas that
are deep and intimate. It is a relationship of trust and
mutual respect. Unlike most physicians, she does not
fear that her professionalism will be threatened by a degree of intimacy with the women who have come to her
for help. She is willing to be called by her given name, even
as she addresses the birthgiver by hers. She does things
with, not *to* the person giving birth. The midwife is also a
teacher in the best sense of the word in that she helps the
birthgiver towards ever greater self-knowledge.[16]

Holy Listening is a testimony to one woman's life experience. Guenther uses categories that come naturally to
someone who has invited guests into her home, who has
worked as a teacher, and who has given birth to and raised
children. Writing about women and their ministry in spiri-

tual direction, Guenther shows how the different attitudes and experiences they bring come both from natural distinctions between men and women and from centuries of conditioning. Women are accomplished listeners: for generations they have been expected to be there for other people. Women can listen maternally in a way that reassures. Women come to the ministry of spiritual direction as outsiders, which helps them in their work with people who are disaffected or have experienced rejection. Women bring their experience of waiting and their need for patience to accompanying others on their journey:

> In their instinctively murmured words of comfort, mothers do not deny the pain, uncertainty, even the terror of life. They simply remind the child—and themselves—that at the deepest level it truly is all right. We can do this as spiritual directors, not in false cheeriness or denial, but by our own steadfastness. If *we* believe with Julian that, in spite of everything, it will be all right, we need not say the words. We can embody them. Finally a great learning from motherhood is the realization that we have our children only on loan, that they are not really "our" children. It's good to remember that we have directees on the same kind of sacred trust.[17]

In *Women Speak: of God, Congregations and Change* historian Joanna Bowen Gillespie takes a different approach to women's sense of the spiritual life. Part of her work has been to listen carefully to the stories of women in the context of their Episcopal church communities, and from that to illustrate some new ways in which women's consciousness is breaking through old, established patterns of church life and thinking:

One of the arenas in which women's changing consciousness has been most fertile—at the same time generating mountains of resistance—is religion. Protestant and Roman Catholic Christianity is being dramatically reshaped through a significant body of feminist theology, writings that open up once-standard terms of faith, ethics and polity to the incorporation of historic female experience....New or reclaimed structures and language, new imaginative formulations are bubbling into consciousness and print. But to date the least studied, least known element in the process of religious change is that involving the female segment of mainline church members in the United States.

Perhaps not surprisingly in view of what we have seen as a lack of spiritual formation in the church, practical work has been emphasized as the natural and proper expression of women's commitment to the church:

In clerically hierarchical churches such as the Roman Catholic, the Episcopal or the Lutheran, women's cultivation of their own inner lives has rarely been given priority. Also, among many Protestant women there is a dread of sounding glib about something as personal as one's soul....Also related to this inhibited spiritual vocabulary were the modest claims the women made for their own spiritual insight and authority. At least in conversation with us, this hardworking, committed group gave "work" rhetorical precedence over everything else.

Yet Gillespie notes a deeper strand in the spirituality of the women with whom she talked, recognizing that there are four dimensions of the soul quest which draw women to a religious community: the search for a direct experience of God; surviving change in lifelong religious habit; the longing for a community that allows deep sharing of ultimate truths; and the congregation as a theological reality.[18]

A study entitled *Episcopal Women: Gender, Spirituality and Commitment in an American Mainline Denomination* surveys attitudes in four different kinds of parish churches. Episcopal women of different generations speak of what it means to belong to a church and to live as a Christian. Again the survey shows the traditional pattern with different positions held by men and women within the Episcopal Church, where till recently the management structures have been a male preserve. For the older woman religion meant working practically for the church. The contrast with younger women is marked. For instance, regarding the spiritual life,

younger women in all four parishes disagreed with the statement *"My spirituality is private and not generally talked about with others."* In all four parishes, the generational divide between the two younger generations and the older one was sharply visible on the issue of privacy and spirituality....Older women regarded religious membership as activity; one's interior life was no one else's business.

Things are changing fast. Women who have their own professional work no longer have the time (or even the need) to be occupied in activities around the parish. In the altered climate the distinctive cast of women's spirituality is also gaining recognition:

Perhaps *the* great untapped source for renewal in congregations is the endlessly questing heart of its generations of women. In many locations women have yet to be perceived as a genuine part of "the whole church" by leaders either in their own congregations or at the national organizational level. But the women-in-the-pew in our study are increasingly less willing to accept beliefs and practices on prescription. They are finding and creating their own space within the institution. Our research uncovered amazing pockets of devotion and spiritual depth in all three generations.[19]

Endnotes

1. Nels Ferre, ed., *The Spiritual Letters of Father Hughson* (London and Oxford: Mowbray, 1952), vii.

2. Shirley Hughson, OHC, *Spiritual Guidance* (West Park, N.Y.: Holy Cross Press, 1948), 4.

3. Adam Dunbar McCoy, OHC, *Holy Cross: A Century of Anglican Monasticism* (Wilton, Conn.: Morehouse-Barlow, 1987), 182.

4. Ferre, *Spiritual Letters*, 10; 36; 53; 214; 15; 181.

5. G. Congreve and W. H. Longridge, eds., *The Letters of Richard Meux Benson* (London: Mowbray, 1916), 255.

6. *Ibid.*, 310.

7. Quoted in Martin Smith, SSJE, ed., *Benson of Cowley* (Cambridge,Mass.: Cowley Publications, 1983), 81.

8. *Ibid.*, 20.

9. R. M. Benson, *Benedictus Dominus: A Course of Meditations for Most Days of the Year* (London: J. T. Hayes, 1876).

10. *Letters of Benson*, 14.

11. *Ibid.*, 242.

12. Urban T. Holmes III, *Spirituality for Ministry* (San Francisco: Harper & Row, 1982), 184.

13. Kenneth Leech, *Soul Friend*, 2nd ed. (London: Darton Longman & Todd, 1994), from the foreword.

14. Tilden Edwards, *Spiritual Friend* (New York: Paulist, 1980), 99-100.

15. Rachel Hosmer, *My Life Remembered: Nun, Priest, Feminist* (Cambridge, Mass.: Cowley Publications, 1991), from the foreword.

16. Margaret Guenther, *Holy Listening: The Art of Spiritual Direction* (Cambridge, Mass.: Cowley Publications, 1992), 13; 44; 89.

17. *Ibid.*, 123.

18. Joanna Bowen Gillespie, *Women Speak: of God, Congregations and Change* (Valley Forge, Penn.: Trinity Press International, 1995),. 2; 21; 3.

19. Catherine M. Prelinger, ed., *Episcopal Women: Gender, Spirituality and Commitment in an American Mainline Denomination* (New York: Oxford University Press, 1992), 218.

Chapter 7

Spiritual Direction and Personal Growth

Spiritual direction and counseling are closely linked. They share common ground, but at the same time they are different arts or disciplines. Counseling is a way of helping people cope with a crisis in their life, usually a specific problem or problems that involve frequent meetings over a relatively short period of time. Spiritual direction, on the other hand, offers a longer term companionship to people who are looking for guidance on their journey of faith. Meetings are less frequent and the conversation often more wide-ranging. In spiritual direction the religious element is always present, while it is not necessarily so in counseling. Both can be described as client-centered, but for spiritual direction God is central to the discussion, too. When both disciplines are practiced well their aim is to enable people to live fully mature lives, part of which consists in accepting responsibility for their own choices. Spiritual direction and counseling also share a common danger: domination by the counselor or director in such a way that someone's ability to choose for him or herself is greatly reduced.

My purpose in this chapter is to trace some of the influences that bear on attitudes and practice among Anglican directors today. In my research into the tradition of spiritual direction I have been looking for those elements that show a continuity of approach. I have enjoyed discovering attitudes in people from the past that are in harmony with what I find among my contemporaries, let alone with my own beliefs. There are, however, plenty of differences. Society changes, culture develops, and the passing of centuries alters the way people think, feel, and react, while new expectations and prejudices arise. Nowhere in the field of pastoral counseling is this more obvious than in the way that we in the late twentieth century make judgments about human behavior.

Sigmund Freud's discovery of the importance of the unconscious is a watershed in the story of this change. In the hundred years since he began to expose the hidden forces that shape many actions and reactions in all our lives, there has been a shift of attitude among Christians in general and among pastors in particular. We are attempting to move away from judgmental moralizing towards an attempt to understand and heal the psychic wounds that drive errant behavior. The writings of Carl Jung, moreover, seem to offer a way of looking at personality that is more sympathetic to the Christian position; in many of his images and much of his language there is a religious slant. His description of the different categories of temperament into which individuals fall is part of the common language of many directors through the later models developed by Isabel Myers and Kathryn Briggs.

I am well aware that before Freud there were confessors, directors, and spiritual friends who by grace, instinct, and compassionate understanding of human beings were able to mediate healing to the damaged depths of men and women who sought their help. I think, for instance, of the way two Victorians I wrote about earlier, Edward King and Harriet Monsell, so clearly and lovingly respected the whole humanity of the people with whom they worked, though without in any way compromising their own well-defined Christian principles. But it is only in this century that pastors have begun to accept the discoveries about human nature that come from the study of psychology and its associated therapies, and to use them as a resource in accompanying souls on their journey.

When people in earlier times asked for help with their problems, the advice they were given tended to be either religious—focused on renewed prayer and devotion—or moralistic, with suggestions for greater personal effort to behave better, often in the form of practical tips. Much of the correspondence in the different collections of nineteenth-century spiritual letters seems to be about scruples. The responses certainly give good, sensible advice, but for a modern reader it seems strange that they rarely touch on either the low self-esteem or the depression that often lies at the root of the problem.

The link between the physical, the emotional, and the spiritual was well known, of course. Although no one would list him among the leading examplars of spiritual directors, I find Sydney Smith's advice about depression in a letter of 1820 to a woman of his acquaintance, Lady Morpeth, very much of a piece with good Anglican pastoral practice. It is compassionate, full of common sense, and, as you would expect from one of the great wits of all time, humorous. He wrote:

Nobody has suffered more from low spirits than I have done—so I feel for you. 1st. Live as well as you dare. 2nd. Go into the shower-bath with a small quantity of water at a temperature low enough to give you a slight sensation of cold. 3rd. Amusing books. 4th. Short views of human life—not further than dinner or tea. 5th. Be as busy as you can. 6th. See as much of those friends who respect and like you. 7th. And of those acquaintances who amuse you. 8th. Make no secret of low spirits to your friends but talk of them freely—they are always worse for dignified concealment. 9th. Attend to the effect tea and coffee produce upon you. 10th. Compare your lot with that of other people. 11th. Don't expect too much from human life—a sorry business at the best. 12th. Avoid serious novels, melancholy, sentimental people, and everything likely to excite feeling or emotion not ending in active benevolence. 13th. Do good, and endeavour to please everybody of every degree. 14th. Be as much as you can in the open air without fatigue. 15th. Make the room where you commonly sit gay and pleasant. 16th. Struggle by little and little against idleness. 17th. Don't be too severe upon yourself, or underrate yourself, but do yourself justice. 18th. Keep good blazing fires. 19th. Be firm and constant in the exercise of rational religion. 20th. Believe me, dear Lady Georgina, Very truly yours, Sydney Smith.[1]

With regard to spiritual guidance and psychological insight, we have already discussed Somerset Ward and his distinctiveness as a spiritual director. One of the benefits that those who came to him for counsel received was Ward's acceptance and use of insights from psychology. Prayer was the major ingredient in his direction and common sense was important, too, but he also realized that the new understanding of the underlying causes of human attitudes and behavior was an essential element in his work.

For him the work of the director was to diagnose the hindrances to the soul's contact with God. The two principal hindrances he identified were sin and fear. Ward understood sin as a choice made by the will that sprang from the dominance of self-love in the soul. The remedy for it was repentance, turning from darkness to light to receive forgiveness, followed by amendment of life. But he was well aware of the emotional factors that lie behind sin. In the early stages of his work with people he was careful to find out about their psychological nature and family background.

The danger presented by fear was part of his own experience and he knew its power, because he suffered for forty years from claustrophobia. In handling fear, Ward taught that it was important first to recognize and name the fear and then to exercise faith in the face of it. His experience as a spiritual director taught him that the six most common forms of fear were the fear of human blame, criticism, or injury; the fear of guilt, incurring God's severity; fears about health; the fear of sex; the fear of inadequacy; and the fear of insecurity.

> There is only one medicine that can produce an absolute cure, and that is a complete and overwhelming faith and simple trust in the power of God, in His will and ability to make of every happening in life a means of ultimate welfare and happiness.[2]

In spiritual direction he offered suggestions for prayer and small acts suited to the different fears that were designed to deepen trust. However, when he saw that someone's problem was a psychological one, he was ready to refer him or her to the specialized help of a psychiatrist. One of his contemporaries wrote that Somerset Ward's gifts of discernment showed themselves above all in helping his directees with the crippling effects of fear.

In evaluating Somerset Ward's importance from the vantage point of today, when counseling of different sorts is widely available, it is important to recognize that the spiritual counsel he offered differs from much that is offered today in not being problem-centered:

> Its business was to aid the "Pilgrim's Progress." Nor was it client-centered, except in the sense that it respected the client and the client's freedom and defended his or her own integrity. It was rather God-centered. There was no concealment of its Christian orientation. Both parties were seeking not just what is right and good but also seeking the One who alone gives the ability to carry out what is right and good.[3]

The Pursuit of Health

Christopher Bryant, SSJE, who lived for many years at the London house of the Society of St. John the Evangelist, was one the many Anglican religious to exercise a formative ministry in spiritual direction. Towards the end of his life (he died in 1985 at the age of eighty) Bryant wrote a number of important books that drew on his own spiritual journey and his insights into the links between the Christian tradition and the teaching of Carl Jung. Well aware that the meaning of Jung's language about God and belief could be at variance with traditional Christian usage, he was nevertheless convinced of the need to draw on the truths that he and other psychologists offered. "Psychology," he wrote in *The Heart in Pilgrimage,*

> can neither prove nor disprove the truths of faith. But it can help contemporary men and women, whether believers or not, to take Christian doctrine seriously by showing how closely linked some of it is to empirical experience. It can also help the believer in the practical task of responding to God's summons to him to live out his humanity to the full. It can in particular bring help to the many who, when they try to pray, feel that their

efforts are like a kind of make-believe, lacking reality and depth. One reason for this sense of superficiality is that their praying is too much a matter of conscious thinking and feeling and does not involve their depths, which may be totally out of harmony with what they consciously express. Dynamic psychology, which stresses the powerful influence that unconscious emotions, such as fear, anger, hate or love exert on our conscious thoughts and actions, can shed much light on the inner obstacles to prayer and can enable us to turn what we had thought to be an enemy into an ally.

Writing about spiritual guidance Bryant recognizes that those who consciously and deliberately set out on the Christian pilgrimage have special need of help. At the beginning they need advice about what kind of prayer is suitable for a particular individual at a particular stage of life and Christian development:

> Much the surest test as to whether a person is on the right lines in his prayer is the effect of his prayer in his daily life. Loving attention to God in prayer will issue in a loving concern for others and a growing indifference to a person's own wishes and interests. If there are no signs of this there must be some doubt as to the genuineness of the prayer.

At the same time, he recognizes that the work of direction differs from that of the professional counselor. Bryant emphasizes three qualities of counseling that are important for spiritual guidance as well: empathy, the ability to enter into a kind of emotional rapport with another person; a truthfulness about our feelings in the relationship; and non-possessive warmth.

What other qualities are needed by the spiritual guide? It would be possible to compile such a list of desirable qualities as would deter anyone with the least scrap of modesty from venturing to undertake an office which demands sanctity, learning and supernatural powers of discernment. But in fact people do not set themselves up as spiritual guides as a doctor might put up a brass plate outside his house to tell the public of his availability. For the most part they are pressed into the position by those who discern in them the qualities of insight and sympathy that they desire in a guide of souls.

No one should undertake to guide others on the spiritual journey who is not himself deeply committed to it. Further he should be interested in the theory and practice of the spiritual life. For people vary and one man's path will follow a different route from another's. Without some knowledge of ways other than his own he may lead other people astray.

What will equip the spiritual guide for his work more than anything is his own persevering prayer and his own personal struggle with the forces of darkness, and his effort to bring under the sway of the Spirit the untamed energies of his own being. The study of the Christian tradition of the spiritual life, especially the acknowledged masters of prayer, will enlarge the store of wisdom from which he can draw. The study of modern psychology will help to provide a contemporary language which makes ancient wisdom bright and new. But in the understanding of others, I believe, psychology helps most indirectly. Its primary use for the spiritual guide is to help him to a greater self-awareness. This enlarged knowledge of himself and of his weakness, his vulnerability and his dependence on divine grace will enable him to enter intuitively into an understanding of others and their trials.[4]

Psychotherapy, analysis, and counseling are so much part of the culture in American life that it is no surprise that American writing about spiritual direction places strong emphasis on the psychological element. In his classic discussion of the nature of contemporary spiritual direction and its relationship to counseling and psychiatry, Gerald May writes:

> The psychiatric dimensions of spiritual direction may seem small and insignificant when compared with the overwhelmingly essential movement of the Holy Spirit in people's lives. Yet these psychiatric phenomena are intimately related to the Spirit's movements and they deserve both attention and response....
>
> Spiritual guidance can hardly be called a disorder-focused discipline. It attends far more to growth, completion and fulfillment than to correction of deficiency or loss. Yet historically it has been a part of the "cure of souls" and therefore must involve a caring for people's overall conditions. Clearly this cannot be divorced from a caring for the healing of human minds. An informed "caring for" need not imply a manipulative "taking care of." Since the first publication of *Care of Mind/Care of Spirit*, I have come to view human psychology as the efficiency of one's functioning, and human spirituality as the dynamic process of love in one's life. This perspective helps me appreciate the particular, intimate interweavings of what our language chooses to call body, mind and spirit without having to compartmentalize the human soul. To those who seek to integrate psycho-

logical and spiritual insight in companioning other people, I say this: The real integration must take place in your own heart, not in any theoretical understanding or system models of care. And it must take place not as a categorical act of integration, but as a gentle easing of compartmentalizing thoughts.[5]

The same priority given to the spiritual over against the psychological is evident in the work of Alan Jones. In *Exploring Spiritual Direction* he writes:

One way of distinguishing spiritual direction from therapy is the acknowledged faith commitment of both parties in an atmosphere of reverence and awe. Spiritual direction is an act of worship. There are certain things which Christian obedience requires which place spiritual direction in a markedly different context from therapy. The world view of the Christian is characterized by repentance and conversion. We Christians are called upon to cultivate a turning to the Lord.... Salvation is the deepest form of therapy we can ever know, and Christ has often been understood as therapist in the literal sense of the word: physician. The cross is the medicine that will heal the world.[6]

Another Anglican whose work values the contributions of psychology is Morton Kelsey in his book *Companions on the Inner Way*. The long list of books written by Kelsey covers a wide range of pastoral care, psychology, and healing. In this carefully analytic work with its very systematic presentation Kelsey, in observing what he calls the "meditation boom," claims that in the market place, where all sorts of spiritualities are on offer, the churches have failed to present the gifts of the Christian inheritance. High among these gifts he lists the tradition of the institution, mystical experience, and the centrality of caring. Whereas much of the psychology used in association with spiritual direction follows the Freudian school, Kelsey shows the strong influence that both the writings of Jung and his own personal experience of Jungian therapy have brought to bear upon his spirituality. He does not describe himself as a Jungian, but rather as "a Christian who has found the thinking of Jung helpful in communicating the world view and message of Jesus to seeking, educated modern men and women."

In contrasting the work of directors before and after the coming of psychological awareness, Kelsey writes:

> The great directors of conscience, the great spiritual guides, have had an *instinctive* knowledge of what makes human beings tick, and so they were able to reach other human beings and to facilitate miracles of transformation. However, few of them could pass on their intuitive understanding. The science of psychology is not yet one hundred years old. It has provided an accumulated body of data about how human beings operate. If we would lead others or ourselves upon the spiritual journey it is foolhardy to ignore the findings of the least of modern psychology. It is like going to a hungry third-world country with no knowledge of modern agriculture.

In an earlier book, *Christo-Psychology*, Kelsey had explored the ways Jung awakens Christians to their traditional doctrines and practices. He relates Jung's idea of individuation to the Christian view of the progress of the soul, and his theories of dreams and archetypes to the Christian concepts of revelation and spiritual beings. Kelsey is well aware, however, that there are important differences.

Salvation consists of a "from what," a "to what," and a "how".... Theological or religious writing often gives us a "from what" and a "to what," but is silent about a "how." Most psychological writing, even the best of it, gives considerable insights into a "from what" and a "how," but shies away from presenting a goal or direction or value for our lives. Jung's theories offered no obstacles to the realization that salvation comes only through divine grace, which alone brings about the transformation within us. According to Jung, we cannot grow psychologically unless we grow religiously and we cannot attain our spiritual maturity unless we mature psychologically.[7]

Spiritual Direction and Healing

On a personal note, when I list the influences that have shaped the way I do spiritual direction, I naturally include the people to whom I went for direction myself. Then there are the four years or so that I spent taking a clinical theology course, which is similar to the training Episcopal seminaries require in Clinical Pastoral Education, as well as time I spent in two local branches of the Samaritans, a confidential service providing support to people in crisis. Clinical theology gave me and hundreds of other pastors insight into human psychology and the ways people suffer from mental and emotional illness. The models and the language were a background against which I was able to listen with more awareness to people in crisis who asked for help from the Samaritans.

Clinical theology was the inspiration of Dr. Frank Lake, who had worked as a medical missionary in India. On his return to England he found that the specialty he had developed to meet what he believed to be the biggest scourge in

India, that of human parasites, was little needed back home. He believed that mental and emotional illness could be seen as a similar scourge in British society and so trained as a psychiatrist. Lake was a committed evangelical Anglican and his faith informed his teaching of psychology. Most models of the human mind and the unconscious tend to be the product of medical doctors, so there is a danger that their models are those of recovery from illness rather than of progress towards wholeness. For Lake the norm of the whole, healthy human being was Jesus Christ. Instead of seeing the work of the psychiatrist simply in terms of attacking illness, he saw it rather as helping people to approximate more to the model of wholeness he saw in the human nature of Christ. Clinical theology was the result.

Although by no means without its critics, clinical theology helped bring together two ways of working with people. Clergy trained in academic and pastoral theology were made aware of psychological knowledge and helped by insights into their own lives as well as those of others. Combining insights and skills from both disciplines developed their ability as pastors. Since the 1960s and 1970s there has been much growth in the area of providing counseling skills for people involved in pastoral ministry. Frank Lake's legacy to the church was to affirm the work of pastors who drew both on the knowledge shared by many schools of psychological research and also on the spiritual resources available to the church. The modern spiritual director cannot ignore the insights and the methods of psychological counseling. Indeed, some directors are themselves qualified counselors or therapists, but in the accompaniment of men and women on their journey of faith there are other means to help.

God heals in many ways. Sometimes it is through human relationships, and the skill and understanding of a counselor, and sometimes through the support of a community. Healing also may come through the sacraments of baptism, eucharist, absolution, the laying on of hands or anointing. Agonizing memories that distort present behavior and broken relationships are also open to God's healing. Past and present wounds that come to light time after time in spiritual direction include rejection in all its many forms, loss and bereavement, fears, problems with self-esteem, anger and guilt, both guilt for actual sins and the kind of neurotic guilt that has power but little basis in past actions. It is part of the gift of a good director to be able to discern when the pain and difficulty a person is experiencing lies within their competence and is properly open to healing through spiritual direction, and when the right course is to ask for the help of counseling or a more intense therapy.

Readers who want to go more deeply into the relationship between the different ways of helping people will find the chapter in Kenneth Leech's *Soul Friend* on "Direction, Counseling and Therapy" extremely helpful. He recognizes that the counseling movement uses many concepts and some language that derive from the Judaeo-Christian tradition: the stress on the centrality of love in therapy, a non-directive approach, and the goal of individual maturity and growth all find a ready acceptance among Christians. Similarly, the group as a focus for counseling has many echoes in church work. There are important distinctions to be made, however, between counseling, social case work, and spiritual direction:

> Certainly the values expressed in the often tedious jargon of the movement are very close to those which appear in the literature of spiritual direction. The pastoral counsellor works with such ideas as empathy, non-possessive warmth, respect for the integrity of the

other, confrontation, support. The Desert Fathers emphasized silence and example, rejected domineering and leadership. The silent witness to authentic living in the hesychast tradition has close parallels with the discipline of analysis. Theodulf wrote of the need for support and salutary counsel. J. N. Grou emphasized mutual respect, courtesy and the need to avoid over-dependence. However, there are some crucial differences between the pastoral counseling movement and the tradition of spiritual direction and it is important to recognize these.

First, the pastoral counsellor's concern has tended to be with states of emotional stress. The ministry of spiritual direction indeed is more important when there are no particular crises. Secondly, the counseling movement has been clinic-based or office-based rather than church-based or community-based. It has therefore lacked the continuous involvement with people in their homes and families which is so essential to pastoral care. Spiritual direction, on the other hand, is firmly located within the liturgical and sacramental framework, within the common life of the Body of Christ. Thirdly, the movement has tended to focus excessively on the problems of individuals, a fault which it has shared with social work and with the church at various stages in its history.

The discipline of direction also shares much of the territory of psychotherapy, psychiatry, and analysis, but with important areas of demarcation. As Leech writes:

The priest cannot ignore the unconscious, and spiritual direction cannot be totally separate from the search for psychological health.... She needs to recognize that all Christian experience involves the experience of disturbance and to look for the movements of the Holy Spirit in the troubled and shaken soul.

In achieving wholeness of life, furthermore, with healing for body and soul, Leech gives full weight to the power of the sacraments, rightly seeing the work of spiritual direction not simply as an individual's personal vocation or skill, but as an integral part of the life and ministry of the whole church.

> At the centre of the Christian tradition are the sacraments, and at the centre of sacramental life is deliverance and healing. Spiritual direction therefore always occurs within a direction of spirit, flowing through the organism of the Body of Christ.

He concludes with a reminder of the supreme importance of listening, both in direction and in the different forms of psychological counseling and therapy, reminding the reader that there is more to listening than hearing and understanding the words with the intellect alone:

> The spiritual guide stands in a close relationship to the human psyche. In the tradition the guide plays a central role in helping individuals to move from one phase to another, to enable them to understand new experiences, and to adjust to them. Spiritual directors and gurus have always been listeners, but the language to which they listen is the "forgotten language" of myths and dreams and symbols, the language of fundamental human experience.[8]

Myers-Briggs and the Enneagram

A tool that in some quarters has come to be regarded as a vital part of the director's equipment is the Myers–Briggs Personality Type Indicator. Working from Jung's analysis of personalities in the 1950s, Isabel Myers and her mother Kathryn Briggs developed a method of identifying sixteen different patterns of people's preferred way of behavior. The language of the eight initial letters has become very useful shorthand in the world of pastoral care in the churches. As well as providing a way to understand and to value differences in personality, it has been used as a help in recognizing people's differing aptitudes for methods of praying.

The four pairs of preferences are E and I, N and S, T and F, and J and P. E and I stand for extrovert and introvert, with the words used in their generally accepted sense. N and S stand for Intuition and Sensation. The S person tends to work in the area of facts and of past experience, while the N person is alive to metaphor and imagery and to what might happen in the future. Jung classified people who choose an impersonal basis for choice as Thinking people and those who choose a personal basis as Feeling. T's are more comfortable with objective judgments, while F's are more comfortable with value judgments. The final pair is the scale between J and P, Judging and Perceiving. J's prefer things to be settled; P's keep options open and fluid. A J person tries to get things done by the deadline that has been set, while for P's deadlines are interesting phenomena that do not really impinge on their lives.

By using a carefully constructed questionnaire it is possible to recognize where someone's preferred pattern of behavior lies on these four scales and to recognize traits in his or her personality that are shared by others who are in a similar place. Shorthand use of the letters gives a language in which to talk about people's preferred attitudes and ways of acting. An INFJ, for instance, will be recognizably different from an ESTP.

This indicator is very useful in creating a kind of geography by which to understand the human landscape. It has the real gift of helping people to recognize and value their own nature. It enables them to see that the way they are is a natural and genuine way of being human, rather than being different from other people and therefore wrong. It can enlighten and affirm. For example, in a busy, achievement-oriented society, notice how many people apologize for being introverts.

It is not only people's strengths that are important. As well as noting their preferred way of behavior the Myers-Briggs also shows what Jung called their "shadow," that part of the temperament that lies fallow or hidden and yet is there to be recognized and helped to grow. This recognition may be of great value in spiritual direction.

With all its positive aspects it has to be recognized that the MBTI can be open to misuse. When it is taken to be prescriptive rather than descriptive it can lead to all sorts of trouble. Kenneth Leech underlines this danger when he refers to Myers-Briggs as "astrology for the middle classes." He notes the dangers posed by the

> uncritical and simplistic adaptation of certain quasi-therapeutic tools. The most obvious example of this is the use of the Myers-Briggs Personality Type Indicator. This grid of sixteen personality types, based on a rather questionable theory of temperament, has rapidly become *de fide* in parts of the spirituality circuit.[9]

When behavior is excused on the grounds that it is predetermined, that is a distortion of the truth. To realize that we are of a certain type does not relieve us from the responsibility of making our own decisions, nor does it mean that we have to behave in a way that is expected from people of that type.

In *Prayer and Temperament*, Chester P. Michael and Marie C. Norrisey use the categories of classical methods of prayer—Ignatian, Augustinian, Franciscan, and Thomistic—and link them with the four main Myers-Briggs temperament groupings. Their work has the great value of recognizing and describing in great detail the different ways in which people find it natural to pray, using different aspects of their whole nature. They recognize the dangers of forcing people to use unsuitable ways of praying:

> Bad experiences with a type of prayer which is unsuited to one's temperament will build up a bias against that type of prayer. Often this prejudice is toward a distorted version of the prayer form. Whenever one particular method of prayer is recommended as the one and only type of prayer for everyone, a negative attitude toward that kind of prayer soon arises. There is no one form of prayer that is best for everyone and for every given occasion. Denying the value of other forms of prayer deprives us of the spiritual riches available to us when we use all four functions and all four attitudes. This is why we recommend the use of all the different methods of prayer which the Christian tradition has developed during the past twenty centuries.

I have met people who become concerned about not praying according to their "type." There is a danger in seeing these descriptive categories as defining the way people ought to behave, rather than as preferred ways of behaving. Michael and Norrisey are careful to make this distinction clear:

> Everything said in this book about the relationship of temperament and prayer needs to be taken with certain reservations. The conclusions drawn are never to be

taken absolutely. They are only somewhat true and somewhat applicable. The rule is only to try out the suggestions. If they work for you and help deepen your prayer life and your relationship with God, then make use of them. God can and frequently does directly intervene in our lives in His own way. We must keep ourselves open to whatever helps we can get from every possible source. The study and knowledge of temperament and type is one of these helps.[10]

The origins of another tool, the Enneagram, are unknown, although its roots may lie in the Sufi tradition of Islamic spirituality. In itself the Enneagram is the figure of a nine-pointed star enclosed in a circle. Used as a diagram for describing types of people with different sorts of personalities it has found wide acceptance in many parts of the church. First introduced into the West by Gurdjieff as he fled the Russian revolution to find refuge in France, it was developed by his followers and in particular by Ouspensky. In the 1970s Oscar Ichazo, a Bolivian, offered the symbol as a paradigm for understanding different aspects of human nature, and since then it has been used in the church as a way of identifying nine particular types of personality.

These nine types, known simply by their number, can be described by identifying specific compulsions that belong to each group of people. These are a response to particular fears that come from life's earliest experience and lead a person to develop distinctive ways of avoidance that shape their preferred attitudes. So, to outline it very briefly, *ones* avoid anger and strive for perfection in what they do, *twos* avoid recognizing that they have needs and instead make a point of being helpful to others, and *threes* avoid failure and work hard for success in their lives. *Fours* avoid ordinariness by seeing themselves as special, *fives* avoid emptiness by trying to amass knowledge, *sixes* avoid deviance and are firmly tied to regulations, and *sevens* avoid pain and exhibit strong optimism and enjoyment. *Eights* avoid weakness and take pride in being strong people, whereas *nines* avoid conflict and are concerned for peace, both within themselves and among those with whom they are in contact. A further grouping can be made according to the preferred centers that people draw upon for functioning with conscious energy. These are the gut center, which draws on instincts and habits; the heart center, with its feelings and emotions; and the head center, which is strong on thinking and reflection. Grouped under the gut center are numbers eight, nine, and one; the heart takes numbers two, three, and four; and the head numbers five, six, and seven.

As with the Myers-Briggs Personality Type Indicator, it is impossible to present the Enneagram fairly here because it is a way of understanding and relating to people that needs time and dialogue to enter into. It may be important as a possible tool for the work of spiritual direction in accompanying personal change and development, rather than simply being a static model of personality typing:

> The Enneagram certainly is a model, in fact a very precise and complex model. It is, however, more than that. Many people have been introduced to it as a "self-knowledge" system. It is this. However, if we expect that knowledge to be merely intellectual we will unduly limit the Enneagram's potential. It is also meant to be an experiential tool, one that opens us more completely to the processes of our lives, one that offers us a way, not simply of understanding human transformation, but also of helping us to *enter into* the process of transformation. In utilizing either the language of transformation or conversion we must still affirm a basic premise. As a

tool for the life journey the Enneagram must be experiential. Its fruitfulness as a means of leading people closer to God and more in touch with their true selves will ultimately not be what it teaches them *about* themselves, although of course this is not inconsequential. Its fruit will lie in how well it leads them beyond themselves to encounter the greater forces of life and the very mystery of God.[11]

Prayer and Temperament

In coming to recognize and value the different ways people pray, Somerset Ward used the concept of *attrait*—"attraction"—to explore the ways people are drawn to pray one way rather than another. As they stand, the three categories he developed—institutional, intellectual, and mystical—omit a large part of what it means to be a human being in prayer. In his dealings with people Somerset Ward gave full weight to the importance of emotions, feelings and instincts, but not in this scheme of prayer. Perhaps the quick and pervasive growth of psychological understanding and the work of counseling in the area of the emotions means that today the affective side of prayer is more highly valued than before, not that it has ever been completely ignored in the past.

In spiritual direction I have found it helpful to offer a simple "mind map" of the ways in which people pray. My map is really about what people do when they give time to praying. Or perhaps more accurately it is about what happens when they pray, because there is a vital element in all the different sorts of praying that is not finally due to the person praying but is of God's gift. Grace happens; it is not something that I do or achieve.

The map is divided into four major quadrants, and the first of these I call *words and systems*. It covers the area of prayer that Somerset Ward called *institutional*. It thrives on some formality. Public worship is an important feature: going to church, worshiping, and praying with others are activities that energize many Anglicans. For this temperament, private prayer also is often formal: "saying prayers" is an accurate description, whether set prayers are read or said aloud, or formulated silently in the mind. Books of prayers are helpful; sometimes people of this temperament make up their own collection of prayers to read or to learn by heart.

I use the word *system*, but perhaps *pattern* would be better for some people. They enjoy order and find real value in doing the same thing in prayer: "What I always do when I pray is...." Many people were taught to pray using the acronym ACTS, for Adoration, Confession, Thanksgiving, and Supplication. Lists are valuable for people who pray this way, such as the intercession lists that come from the diocese or from missionary societies giving people and causes to pray for regularly. There are lists that people write for themselves of friends and family, people who are ill, and their concerns in the world in which they live. The lists can be organized for daily prayer or for weekly or, like the Anglican Cycle of Prayer, following the calendar through the days of the month.

I have a vivid memory of a conversation with someone about the way she prayed. As we went through the map, she said that the only part that made sense to her was the part about Words and Systems. When I asked her what she did for a living, she told me she was an office administrator. It does not always follow that work and prayer are as neatly aligned as that, but it is unusual for a person's faculties in prayer to be totally at odds with their main interests and skills in the rest of their life.

"Chatting with my friend God" is how one person described her going through the day. She found herself referring to God things that happened, problems she met, and people she was bothered about. Prayer like this is a conversation either spoken or formed in the heart with a God who cares and listens. Occasionally there is the sense that God replies.

Calling the next category *intellectual*, as von Hügel and Somerset Ward did, bristles with difficulties. It immediately calls up images of university professors and intense conversations between highly intelligent people. So I prefer to call this section *thinking* because that is something everybody does whether they consider themselves intellectual or not. By thinking I mean using "the front of your mind" to make sense of a problem, to figure something out. It is using your conscious mind to get in touch with God.

In the language of classical spirituality this is the area of meditation. People use their minds to think about their lives and to think about God and their relationship with him. Often people take passages in the Bible and study them to see what they have to tell them about God and their own lives. For some people an important part of prayer is this time spent with a Bible passage and a commentary, entering into its background, its meaning, and how what the writer has to say applies to them. It could be trying to understand the meaning of a story from one of the gospels or facing up to the huge problem of evil in the world over against the belief in a loving creator God. Or it could be opening before God in prayer all the factors that have to be taken into account before making a major decision about a job. This way of prayer also includes reviewing before God what has happened in the day and looking forward to engagements and events that are expected to happen in the day ahead—the prayer of practical planning and reflection.

Under the heading of *senses, feeling, and images* I group all sorts of features in praying that are neither words nor thoughts. It is those ways of praying that use the imaginative and affective faculties. Prayer and the physical senses includes both how someone is led into prayer, how their prayer is affected by what they receive from their senses, and how they express their prayer in creative ways. Looking at a glorious sunset; gazing up into the vaulting of a great cathedral; being moved to a deeper plane by a chorus from an oratorio or a violin solo; the reminder of holiness that may come with the scent of incense; the effect on us that comes from kneeling on a low stool—the possibilities are endless. They underline the truth that prayer is a concern of the body, not simply a question of the human soul searching for God. A whole person is engaged in the enterprise and that includes the physical. So for some people it is the senses that lead them to prayer—the senses of taste, touch, smell, hearing—and for others it is the body that expresses prayer through painting, movement, song, making music. For many thousands of years people have expressed their prayer in song or with a musical instrument.

By *feelings* I mean our affective, emotional side. Again, this is both passive and active. The affective side of our nature is either a way into prayer, a way of praying, or a way of experiencing the effect of prayer. It is useful to note how someone is emotionally moved to pray, how their prayer is affected by their feelings, and also how prayer is expressed in and through their emotional responses. Feelings like warmth, loss, and emptiness, love or anger are very common in people who pray. Fear is a well-known spur to prayer, as are joy and gratitude.

One of the important lessons to be learned from the great spiritual teachers of the past is that the purpose of prayer is not to achieve good feelings. Warmth, joy, and an awareness of closeness to God are gifts God gives us sometimes, but we do well to grow out of loving God for the good feelings he gives us into a love of God for who he is. Among the early hermits in the Egyptian desert tears were sometimes regarded as a mark of sanctity. I doubt whether we would say the same, but certainly one aspect of the relationship between prayer and the emotions is how we are able to own and perhaps to release our feelings in prayer. It is always worth noting how people feel in prayer because feelings are more immediate and direct than thoughts. They often indicate what is deepest, what God is doing in someone's life.

Images refer to our use of imagination, fantasy, and ability to daydream. When people talk loosely about Ignatian meditation, they usually mean a way of prayer in which the imagination and fantasy are given full play. Meditating on a story about Jesus in the gospel, some find they can slip easily into this kind of praying and move from a sense of the warmth of the sun by the Sea of Galilee, the smell of the dried fish on the nets, and the sand crunching beneath their toes into a personal conversation with the Lord whom they meet on the shore. Others, for whom this is not their way, find it impossible.

Images can also be a bridge leading into the fourth and contemplative way of praying. In the prayer of *attitudes*, people find that they use the other ways of prayer less and less. When the unknown author of the fourteenth-century *Cloud of Unknowing* tries to help his pupil in the art of contemplation, "unknowing" does not simply mean a lack of intellectual understanding or activity. It points to a generally more passive way of prayer. St. John of the Cross speaks of the ligature that cuts off the ability to think or feel when someone is praying in a contemplative way.

So in this way of praying the key is our *attitude* towards being available for God, waiting for God, being empty. The use of the Jesus prayer or centering prayer may be helpful, but the prayer of attitudes is not just a technique to be learned. Because of its nature such prayer is very hard to describe; even images and pictures are very little help. Often when people talk about it they speak very tentatively or use double negatives: "I don't really know how to describe what goes on when I pray. All I can say is that God is not absent."

What is at work on the human side in this prayer is the will. It is simply a matter of choosing to be available. As Reginald Somerset Ward said, "The will is the voice of the soul." It is a way of prayer in which the ideas of gift and acceptance are important, not the effort to achieve. It is prayer from God, or in God.

My prayer map is untidy, with gaps and anomalies. One kind of prayer that I find hard to fit in is charismatic prayer. Sometimes the gift of intense experience in prayer fits most closely in the quadrant of senses and feelings, yet there is at the heart of charismatic renewal the deep belief in God's grace. Charismatic gifts are not achieved; they are given by God. There is for some people a close link with the prayer of attitudes and contemplation: their way of praying is centered on the will to be available for God. Gifts like praying in tongues take the individual into a place that is beyond thinking or using words.

Nor has the map any specific place for sacramental prayer. For many people the heart of their spirituality is the eucharist. What has shaped them is the dying to the old and birth into the new through baptism, and this they relive in Holy Communion. It is in the sacrament that they come into close relationship with God, with Jesus through the Holy

Spirit. My experience is that the way a person prays through the eucharist can follow any of the different paths I have outlined.

Little that I have said about these four ways of praying will be new to anyone who works in spiritual direction, though some may find it helpful to have it set out simply. They will certainly recognize that among the different people they accompany on the journey of faith there are examples of each of the types. It also goes without saying that the right way for people to pray is in the way that works for them. One of the basic beliefs in spiritual direction is that God is at work in someone's life—which means, among other things, that God's grace is at work in their praying. So the director's first job is to identify and to value what is actually happening when the person prays.

Usually someone will be more at home in one or perhaps two of the four quadrants than in the others. To have a good balance there should something of each quadrant, and this may mean that the director will feel it right to encourage some new ways of praying to fill the gaps. What an experienced director will also recognize is that people change. It is not uncommon for people to start to pray in words and patterns because that is what they have been taught. Then in time they may find that something goes "flat" in their praying. They find they are using other faculties to pray but feel guilty because they do not keep up with the old patterns or say the prayers they were taught to use. It is here that spiritual direction classically comes into its own. The wise director is in a position to help them to recognize whether this is a sign that spiritual development is taking place and to encourage them in new ways.

This is particularly true when someone is moving into contemplative prayer. It is then that the spiritual upheaval seems most acute, when someone who has been praying in an active way begins to find that they are being led to do less and simply to be there for God or with God. Often people are afraid that the lack of feelings or the deadness of prayer is their own fault and blame themselves for it. That may be true—there may be a refusal of God or some serious and unrepented sin that is causing a block. Or, more usually, it may be that change and development are taking place. Spiritual muscles are beginning to work in reverse. It is here that the help of a director can be most useful in discerning what is happening and how to react to it.

Endnotes

1. Hesketh Pearson, *The Smith of Smiths* (London: Hogarth Press, 1984), 164.

2. Reginald Somerset Ward, *A Guide for Spiritual Directors* (London: Mowbray, 1957), 20.

3. John Townroe, Somerset Ward Memorial Lecture, Guildford Cathedral, October 3, 1992.

4. Christopher Bryant, SSJE, *The Heart in Pilgrimage* (Wilton, Conn.: Morehouse, 1994), 21; 117; 128.

5. Gerald G. May, *Care of Mind / Care of Spirit: A Psychiatrist Explores Spiritual Direction*, 2nd ed. (San Francisco: Harper, 1992), ix, xvi.

6. Alan Jones, *Exploring Spiritual Direction: An Essay on Christian Friendship* (New York: Seabury Press, 1982), 48.

7. Morton Kelsey, *Companions on the Inner Way* (New York: Crossroad, 1983), 40-41; 7.

8. Kenneth Leech, *Soul Friend*, 2nd. ed. (London: Darton, Longman & Todd, 1994), 95; 101; 117; 129.

9. Kenneth Leech, *The Tablet*, 22 May 1993.

10. Chester P. Michael and Marie C. Norrissey, *Prayer and Temperament*, (Charlottesville: The Open Door, 1984),19; 10.

11. Bernard Tickerhoof, TOR, *Conversion and The Enneagram* (Denville, N.J.: Dimension Books, 1991), 142.

Chapter 8

Training in Spiritual Direction

The title of this chapter immediately raises a number of questions. Who should be trained as spiritual directors? How do we train them? What kind of qualification does the training give them? But there is also a prior question underlying these. What qualifies someone to be a spiritual director?

From its start with the desert fathers and mothers right through to our day, the Christian tradition of spiritual direction has been clear. Sanctity is the first qualification for working as a director, a personal holiness that both attracts people to seek advice and is the main resource for helping them. The second obvious but important condition that needs to be satisfied before anyone can work as a director is that people seek them out. Not only holiness is required, but *recognized* holiness. By holiness I do not necessarily mean anything exalted—not Sainthood with a capital S. I mean a commitment to the journey of faith and prayer, a deep desire for God, and a pattern of life that both reflects and develops that desire. In a meeting with a person who has what it takes to be a good director something "comes across" that inspires confidence; on reflection, you realize that the Third Person is there all along in the conversation.

That sounds imprecise, but spiritual direction does not tolerate over-definition. It is clear to me, however, that directors do emerge and are discovered. It is a matter of gifts and grace, not a matter of personal ambition or other people's planning. It follows, then, that training for spiritual direction has to be different from forms of training for many other kinds of work. There is a real danger that the edges may get blurred between the need for deepening a person's life in God and for technical training in the skills of this art.

This danger becomes very clear if we look again at the words and play language games. To "direct" is to "point in a certain direction." From the same Latin word comes the French *diriger*, to steer. Driving schools teach people to drive, to control the speed and direction of a car. When the instructor has done good work, the learner takes a test, passes, and is licensed to drive a car on the highway. The work of spiritual direction is altogether different from driving a car, and every effort must be made to avoid using the model of mechanistic skill-training in preparing people to undertake the ministry.

In 1993 Kenneth Leech opened a debate with a sharp article entitled "Is Spiritual Direction Losing Its Bearings?" In it he acknowledged the growth in interest in spiritual direction in the fifteen years since he wrote *Soul Friend:*

> Spiritual direction is "in" again with a vengeance. There are workshops, institutes, cassettes, courses, books galore. Institutes and networks have grown up to train people, mainly lay women and men, as spiritual directors. There has been considerable attention to the role of women. All this has been exciting, healthy, positive, hopeful. Why then am I worried?

I am worried, first, that spiritual direction is being seen as more important than it is. It is, after all, one ministry among others. Directors play an important but quite lowly and limited function within the wider context of pastoral care and theological formation.

I am worried that this ministry is being professionalized and seen as a specialist ministry in a way that is potentially extremely dangerous. People are being "accredited" with certificates, diplomas and doctorates in spiritual direction by the many institutes and departments that have sprung up.

I stand by my insistence in 1977 that spiritual direction is not essentially a ministry for specialists and professionals, but part of the ordinary pastoral ministry of every parish and every Christian. Even more so do I stand by my suggestion that the role of "training" is extremely limited, and that this ministry is essentially a by-product of a life of prayer and growth in holiness. Part of our work is to discover, help and affirm the work of direction that is already being done by unknown people who do not write books or run courses.[1]

Leech strikes a note that rings very true to the Church of England's ethos and highlights some of the differences between practice there and in the Episcopal Church. There is that element of homeliness, practicality, and common sense that must be held in tension with an increasing stress on "professionalism." I share Leech's fear that success in learning techniques might be thought to give those who acquire it the right to be known as a spiritual director. All my instincts and experience tell me to look for signs of God's grace that are not subject to grades or degree programs.

This is not by any means to say that the director has no need of training. The whole model of spiritual direction is one of education, training, coaching, travelling together—whatever language you want to use. One person is there to help another grow, develop, learn, and mature as a Christian. So the teacher, trainer, coach, or companion needs similar help towards maturity in Christ.

The way most people learn anything is from others who know about it. It is the most basic and among the most effective forms of training. Sitting with people while they do what they do is one of the best ways to learn a skill. If someone has been engaged in making up circuit boards for fifteen years, you can do a lot worse than sit beside her and watch how she does it. In pastoral work as well, people reflect the technique of those who trained them. In the intimate ministry of spiritual direction this is especially true: how you have been helped is likely to be the way you help others. Unless you are very aware, it can also mean that you may well pick up blind spots and distortions from the person who has accompanied you. There is a more important and deeper principle involved, however: someone who is offering spiritual direction should be receiving it as well. Openness to spiritual growth in oneself comes before any training in technique. Of course it will vary from individual to individual, but unless it is there in some form, any direction is likely to be futile.

Before we look at formal training courses, we have to recognize that this kind of personal formation of the next generation of directors has been going on quietly among Anglicans for more than a century and a half. With the Oxford movement and the catholic revival came a return in some parts of the church to formal sacramental confession and absolution. Many letters of spiritual advice were written by people like John Keble and Edward King, and we have already taken note of Edward Pusey's edition of Abbé Gaume's treatise for confessors. Coming to our own century, some element of training in spiritual direction has existed in the church since the 1920s. Reginald Somerset Ward gave the courses that led to his *Guide*. The Society of Retreat Conductors was founded in 1927 with the specific purpose of training Anglican clergy in giving Ignatian retreats. In 1937 the retreat house at Stacklands in Kent was built by the society, and until the 1970s it was virtually alone in the Church of England in promoting Ignatian spirituality and training people as directors. However, it is interesting to note that Ignatius Loyola has had his followers in the Church of England since the mid-nineteenth century. W. H. Longridge of the Society of St. John the Evangelist wrote a treatise on *The Spiritual Exercises of St. Ignatius of Loyola* that was published in 1919. His scholarship in Ignatian studies has been widely recognized.

Today a tension exists that is all too apparent in the practice of training for many different areas of ministry, the tension between experiential ways of learning and academic instruction. They should be complementary, but often seem to be in competition. The days when an Oxford or Cambridge degree qualified one for ordination in the Church of England are long past, but school and university have provided a model that still dominates teaching and training. In America particularly the strong emphasis on intellectual education in the training of the clergy has had its effect on spiritual direction; the pursuit of academic degrees is often at the expense of spiritual formation. The basis for theological education lies in an understanding of knowledge inherited from the Enlightenment. Logical thought is all important, at the expense of the knowledge that is contemplative, of spiritual awareness. The faculties of feeling and the will are felt to be inferior, a long way behind the use of the powers of the intellect. A theological education that is seen as an academic discipline leading to the awarding of degrees affords little space for the Christian's need to be present to God and to be open to a different way of knowing. The result is that although seminaries show much concern for spirituality and the spiritual development of their ordinands, it is not their main interest.

In a study of education in spirituality and the availability of spiritual direction in seminaries Foster Freeman, whose affiliation is to the Presbyterian Church and the United Church of Christ, writes about his own preparation for ministry:

> I did my first year of studies at Harvard Divinity School and the Swedenborg School of Theology, NY, second and third years at Union Theological Seminary in New York City. By the time I was in my middler year I perceived that the spiritual guidance I hoped to provide eventually to parishioners I not only was not being trained to give but also had not experienced myself.[2]

In support of his own experience Freeman quotes Tilden H. Edwards, whose book on spiritual direction related these findings from a study of a number of seminaries that was undertaken in 1979 and 1980:

> No long-term process of spiritual formation can be assumed in the background of entering students, and perhaps for number of faculty as well.

> Individual conscience has become increasingly important in the context of few or no agreed-upon norms. Students are pressed toward a desire for more ongoing personal spiritual guidance to help them discern the way the spirit is moving in their particular situation and to help with the development and accountability

for a disciplined attentiveness to this grace, individually and corporately.

As this has grown, there appears to be a shortage of faculty/staff persons who feel competence, confidence and call to be such guides.

Participating faculty and staff members mentioned

the serious problem of attending spiritual development amidst the great academic pressures put on students by most curricula, which tend to choke out or remove to the periphery serious concern for an integral faith life.[3]

Freeman also went on to note the strongly intellectual bias of training, although in the early 1970s students became increasingly aware of and vocal about their need for spiritual mentors and help in their own development. Roman Catholic author and religious Sandra Schneiders tells a similar story about the lack of resources for training people in the area of spiritual direction:

When I undertook to teach a course on spiritual direction in 1976 I discovered that there were practically no books in English available on the subject. John McNeill's classic work in comparative history had been reprinted. Merton's little essay, already fifteen years old and more monastic in approach than was suitable for my students, was still available. Jean Laplace's substantively excellent, but somewhat old-fashioned and clerical, treatment of the subject had just been translated from the French. With these exceptions, almost all useful material on spiritual direction was in the form of articles on specific aspects of this ministry appearing with increasing frequency in periodicals devoted to spirituality and religious life....With the appearance the following year of Kenneth Leech's very fine study, *Soul Friend*, perhaps still the best overall treatment available, a veritable publishing phenomenon began.[4]

Advances in the understanding of adult education have improved the church's awareness that men and women learn from reflecting on their experience of life and from their relationships with other people as much as they do from reading books or attending lectures. The tension I have mentioned between the two ways of educating and training is obvious in the field of spiritual direction. Evelyn Underhill's appeal to the Lambeth bishops sixty-five years ago has taken a very long time to bear fruit. If at any time during those two generations, people went to their minister with a spiritual question, it is more than likely that after some conversation he would have offered to lend them a "good book on the subject"—which is so often the Anglican way!

At the time of the Second World War, training in prayer and spirituality was dominated in England by books like F. P. Harton's *The Elements of the Spiritual Life*, written "to give to my brethren of the Anglican Communion what we do not at present possess, a comprehensive study of the Christian spiritual life." First published in 1932, the book was regularly reprinted, clearly valued for its exhaustive presentation of the classical tradition of prayer and spirituality and the theology that underlies it. In the final chapter on "the guidance of souls," Harton asserts that

> an essential part of the ministry of every priest is the guidance of the souls committed to him in their response to the Holy Spirit and their willed participation in that life. Spiritual direction is not the close preserve of a few experts, but an essential part of the responsibility of every priest with a cure of souls.

He underlines his view of the grave responsibility of the director, who

> has to take cognisance of the whole spiritual life of the soul, and show it the way in which it should go in prayer, mortification, the practice of virtue—indeed in every department of life.

This high view of the director's work Harton supports with a quotation from Gilbert Shaw:

> Direction is the art of guiding souls so that they shall respond most readily to their graces.... It implies a settled relationship between director and directed, not merely by way of giving and seeking advice, which would still leave open the private judgement of the one directed, but rather a relationship resulting from prayer and careful search in which the soul has found the "guide of souls" upon whom it feels it can depend. Being sure of this, the soul has adopted the avowed intention of obeying the counsels of that friend.

Whether there are many directors who would openly subscribe to that view of direction today is open to question. But there is no doubt that it describes a relationship between directee and director that is in practice not at all uncommon.

On the qualifications a director needs, Harton is clear:

> The priest's whole ability to guide souls depends upon his being a man of God. Spiritual guidance can only be undertaken by one who is himself humbly seeking to live with and for God: a worldly priest, though he may be popular, is incapable for this work; nor is it sufficient merely to have a good knowledge of human nature nor to be well up in the latest theories of psychology. The di-

rection of souls is the work of the Holy Spirit, and the priest is simply the human medium through whom the Spirit works.

The priest treats souls on the spiritual level and what is important for him is an adequate knowledge of the four closely related branches of theology—dogmatic, moral, ascetical, and mystical. Of these we would stress the third, which should be studied not in little modern books, but in the works of the proved masters.[5]

Certainly the knowledge Harton presupposed was provided in his book in summary form, but to be real and to be of use, it would have to be grounded in practice and experience. A telling insight into the effect of Harton's work comes from the late Terry Holmes, theologian and dean of the School of Theology at the University of the South. In the early eighties he made a survey of twenty clergy and ministers to assess their attitudes to spirituality. In the introduction to his essay he wrote about his own training for ministry:

A retreat master when I was a seminarian told us that if we were marooned on a desert island and could choose to have three books with us, we should choose the Bible, the Book of Common Prayer (an obvious choice for Episcopal seminarians), and Frederic P. Harton's *Elements of the Spiritual Life*. Harton's book is one of those products of Anglo-Catholic scholarship that flourished between the two world wars and consists of a totally non-discriminating assimilation and regurgitation for unsuspecting Anglicans of the worst in post-Vatican I Roman Catholic theology. I do not believe I ever knew more than one or two persons who read it all the way through, although it undoubtedly gathers dust on the shelves of many an Anglican priest's study.[6]

The latest of this type of academic studies is *Spiritual Direction* by Martin Thornton, which was published in 1984 and grew out of the author's work in leading a four-year course in spiritual direction in the diocese of Truro. It is hard to commend it as in any sense representing contemporary good Anglican practice. For all Thornton's assurance of respect for individuals, his approach is systematic and driven by the intellect, showing very little affirmation of God's gifts in people. What often seems lacking is a sense of loving concern for the person, although Thornton sets great store by knowledge as a qualification for the director. "Spiritual direction is a complicated business," he had written earlier,

> a combination of art and science with science the predominant partner. It is the application of theology to the life of prayer. Since prayer as progressive relationship with God in Christ is carried on in the world, it ultimately controls all aspects of life.[7]

In his list of the qualities needed in a director, Thornton includes love, prudence, understanding, human concern, psychological insight, experience, discernment and, at the top of the list, knowledge. This preeminence of knowledge characterizes the book and presumably much of the training courses Thornton led. *Spiritual Direction*'s greatest weakness is its concentration on academic learning to the exclusion of personal skills. Certainly the director needs to have knowledge, as Thornton regularly insists, but the knowledge required is surely *knowledge of* rather than what is offered here in huge quantity, *knowledge about*. The director needs above all to have knowledge of God and knowledge of people, even though neither of these can be in any sense complete in this life. As well as an awareness of these two "knowing" relationships, the director also needs some kind of language in which to talk about them, some kind of pattern or geography within which to make connections and assessments, some way to own them and to communicate them.

Such is the work of theology. Thornton is right to recognize that we have a long and full tradition of past theologies to draw on, but his book has too much of it and too many lists of abstruse technical words. There is an almost total absence of stories about people and their experiences of life, but a superabundance of categories of all kinds into which to put them and their behavior. His repeated image of spiritual direction as dissection is particularly unpleasant. In the chapter entitled "Love on the Slab" Thornton insists that

> the most efficient, creative and ultimately loving way to direct a brother-in-Christ is ruthlessly to split him up, classify and categorize him, according to the classical system of orthodox ascetics.

Nor does he give much weight to the value of people's own experience of God and their search for the means to express it. Thornton acknowledges that he shies away from the personal, saying, "If I am still a little unhappy about 'ministerial skill,' I am even more so with pastoralia presented in the context of autobiography, however venerable the author might be."[8]

In complete contrast to Thornton, though also the fruit of a diocesan training course, is Gordon Jeff's *Spiritual Direction for Every Christian* published in 1987. Jeff states very clearly that an "elitist view of spiritual direction has done immeasurable harm, and has inhibited many Christians from going to talk through where they are with some understanding person." He goes on to outline what direction means in practical terms for most people. Recognizing the vital need to listen and to begin with people where they are, Jeff believes this ministry of guidance should be available for every Christian in every congregation. He is eager to dispel any suspicion that spiritual direction is a hothouse affair:

> As anyone who has done a reasonable amount of directing will know, the greater part of our time is spent on quite simple and basic worries and questions that do not require Thornton's "assault course" training, which sometimes seems to assume that the director is expected to produce "answers." If the director believes that the Holy Spirit is the real director, then there will be an openness to the situation that will not attempt to force a particular way upon the directee.

> So while I believe that Thornton is right to warn us that the director must not force his own way upon the client, and that technical knowledge is a good thing, I should want to have as my key words, even more than knowledge, holiness, sensitivity, insight and trust in the Holy Spirit's guiding into all truth.

In his practical handbook one can find clearly set out the resources that are available to a director and a full account of the kind of training that has helped many directors and rippled out into many parishes and communities. He includes an important chapter on "the outsider" that deals with the experience—increasingly common—of working in spiritual direction at a deep level with people who are sincere in their quest but are not professing Christians. Jeff ends by saying:

What the spiritual director is concerned about, with Christian and outsider alike, is finding ways of taking what we already know in our mind down into the heart, so that it becomes a part of our deepest experience; and the quality of the direction relationship—of any relationship—is one of the most important factors in transferring our faith from head to heart. In the final analysis I believe that the most important thing in direction has relatively little to do with what is said, but a great deal to do with the quality of the relationship between director and directee.[9]

Training and Professionalism

Over the past twenty years courses in spiritual direction have been started in different dioceses of the Church of England, often on the initiative of the diocesan bishop. In Truro Bishop Graham Leonard entrusted Martin Thornton with the task in the 1970s. Both Timothy Bavin on his arrival in Portsmouth from South Africa and Mark Santer on his consecration as Bishop of Kensington encouraged their clergy to have a spiritual director and provided training. Sheila Watson and I established a training course in the Kensington area for beginners in the work. A spiritual direction program called SPIDIR, founded in the early 1980s and led for many years by Gordon Jeff in the diocese of Southwark, is one of the most comprehensive courses and has been much imitated. Almost all the courses in Britain were founded as or have developed into ecumenical events, since it has become self-evident that denominationalism has little or no place in the work of spiritual direction.

Several nationally based courses also exist. All are ecumenical and most of them take place in London. Among the earliest was one based at Heythrop College, under Jesuit leadership, and a second owes its beginning in the early 1980s to a request from Bishop Philip Goodrich, then President of the Association for Promoting Retreats. The latter, in conjunction with the Catholic National Retreat Movement, chaired at the time by Elizabeth Smyth, a religious of the Cenacle, set up a course led by Christopher Lowe of the Community of the Resurrection and Elizabeth Smyth. Some two hundred people from different churches and many parts of the country have completed the three-year part-time training course. Under Raymond Avent, the diocese of London established a center for spirituality at St. Vedast's in the city of London, which runs two-year courses in spiritual direction for several years with an ecumenical team and membership.

What the different courses around the country offer to their students varies considerably. The differences are well illustrated by the names that the Craighead Spirituality Centre in Edinburgh gives to the range of three different courses: Growth in Prayer and Reflective Living, Training in Faith Accompaniment, and Training in Spiritual Direction. Most of the courses describe their work in terms similar to that of the East Midlands SPIDIR, whose stated goal is "to help participants to deepen their own spiritual experiences and awareness as a base from which they can begin to help others."

Basically, the method of training directors is to assist people in their personal growth and to help them to be more aware of their own deepening life of prayer. Some courses indeed set out to do little more than this. Others have the more limited aim of equipping people to accompany others in prayer as, for example, in Guided Weeks of Prayer. In most instances there is a selection process for those who wish to join. Courses that offer more specific training in direction require that members should already be engaged in accompanying others, however informal the setting. Some courses are based on Ignatian principles; the longer ones usually include participants doing the Ignatian spiritual exercises, either in a thirty-day retreat or over a more extended period. Every course emphasizes people working together and the practical experience of accompanying one another. In many there is the opportunity for supervision of the work they are already doing as spiritual directors outside of the course.

Over two hundred institutes have been founded across the United States for training in spiritual direction. Unlike England, where the majority of courses have been founded and are run ecumenically, most are started by one or other of the major denominations. It is the case, however, that in practice Christians from other churches work on their faculties and are welcome as students. Most of them have a basis in Ignatian spirituality and methods of direction. Many them also have a strong psychological orientation, although in a minority there is less emphasis on psychology and more on the tradition stretching back to the desert fathers. Their grounding is firmly in experiential learning and in the importance of the contemplative heart.

The pioneer program is the Center for Christian Spirituality, which is part of The General Theological Seminary in New York. Since it started in 1976 it has offered courses that combine experiential and academic learning to develop the gifts of lay and ordained people to guide others in the life of the Spirit. M.A. (full-time) and S.T.M. (part-time) degrees are awarded. The courses require study of Scripture and theology, of human personality and spirituality, and practical supervision and group work to encourage individuals in their own development and in their work of accompanying others. Candidates for degrees also submit a thesis. Although Anglican in its spirit and practice, the center welcomes participants from other denominations. Participants are expected to be at least thirty years old, with ten years of adult experience in the church.

At a different point on the scale is the Shalem Institute for Spiritual Formation in Washington, D.C. It began in the regular meetings of a contemplative prayer group, whose members combined in 1978 with the Washington Theological Union to offer a course for people called to the ministry of spiritual direction. Now Shalem has a range of courses, including an eighteen-month Personal Spiritual Deepening Program, a one-year Group Leaders Program, and a two-year Spiritual Guidance Program. This last is, like the whole institute, ecumenical. According to its mission statement, it is

> designed to provide resources and support for the ministry of spiritual guidance and to assist people in clarifying their calling to this ministry. Its focus is the ancient Christian practice of spiritual direction, reclaimed, explored, and reenvisoned for our time. Special weight is given to the resources of Christian discernment and contemplative traditions.

The course is comprised of elements of retreat, personal spiritual guidance, reflection on experience in peer groups, reading, papers, and attendance at seminars. The time commitment is an average of thirty-five hours per month month. Although Shalem awards a certificate of completion for each program,

> this is not intended as a certification of the person as a director or validation of one's call to the direction ministry. While an attempt is made to help the person discern that call, we believe that the final confirmation is known in the fruits of the ministry and is clarified

through the Spirit of Truth alive in the director, the directee, and the community of faith.

A more rural retreat center is Stillpoint, which began as an initiative of the Episcopal Diocese of Nashville under the leadership of Elizabeth Canham. Stillpoint is now incorporated as an independent ecumenical course, providing opportunities for learning and prayer for emerging spiritual directors. It describes itself as "a community lured by God into being" and a place of prayer and openness to God. After a foundation year, called Exploring Spiritual Journey and Spiritual Direction, and a further year of development, participants may take the academic and practical course called Intensive Preparation for the Ministry of Spiritual Direction. The commitment is one meeting per month. Contemplative prayer features strongly as a basis for accompanying others, with a link to a near by Benedictine monastery enriching the courses.

The American genius for activity and systematic organization has a bearing on the different attitudes to the training of spiritual directors and to spirituality in general in the Episcopal Church. I notice that many centers advertise their courses under specific labels, whether it is Celtic, Benedictine, Franciscan, or Ignatian. There are systems for sorting and labelling personalities and spiritual tendencies in the Myers–Briggs Personality Type Indicator and the Enneagram. Since the Episcopal Church does not have many religious communities, there is a recognized need for more centers of quiet and reflection in church life to balance the culture of activity and energetic acquisition of knowledge and qualifications.

Spiritual directors in Britain and the United States differ markedly over the question of certification and credentials. In Britain, particularly among Anglicans, spiritual direc-

tors do not advertise nor do they carry business cards, and
it is rare that they expect a fee. In the United States, business cards are not unusual and some sort of certification is
important. To some extent this is the result of the high regard that Americans have for qualifications of all kinds; it
is simply part of a culture that values self-improvement
and upward mobility. English Anglicans find it strange that
this habit obtains among the clergy, too, with certificates of
ordination hanging on the rector's wall, so it is not surprising that spiritual directors come under the same influences.

These attitudes are not universal, however. Well-known
author and director Margaret Guenther describes spiritual
direction as an art for amateurs:

> The amateur is one who loves, loves the art that she
> serves, loves and prays for the people who trust her,
> loves the Holy Spirit who is the true director in this
> strange ministry called spiritual direction. The amateur
> is nervous about hanging up a nameplate or taking an
> advertisement in the Yellow Pages. The amateur waits
> for others to name his gift and may find out quite acci-
> dentally his calling to this ministry.[10]

Her stance is echoed by Bishop Michael Marshall:

> The last thing in the world a spiritual director claims to
> be is an expert. He or she (and this is clearly a ministry
> that has been undertaken both by men and women, lay
> as well as ordained, throughout the centuries) merely
> seeks to come alongside another pilgrim and to accom-
> pany that disciple on the Way that leads to fullness of
> life and to holiness of life.[11]

The status of spiritual directors and the debate over professionalism focuses on two areas, money and accreditation. In an early number of *Presence*, the journal of Spiritual

Directors International, Bill Creed wrote two fictional letters in reply to the question,

> Why is it that I am "worth" anywhere between $5 and $20 for an hour as a spiritual director, when a therapist gets between $40 and $100, a masseuse $50, etc? When I taught piano I received $35 to $50 an hour. Why, when the Spirit calls me to this incredibly wonderful work of spiritual guidance, am I penalized for it?

The first imagined reply is from someone who considers spiritual direction a ministry:

> Now you have begun to understand the great price you are paying because you have chosen to respond to the Spirit's work. The "world" does not value spiritual direction and spiritual directors do not value the "world's" values. Doing this ministry always brings its own rewards but these rewards are not financial; rather, they reward our souls and nourish our world's spirit. Spiritual direction, like preaching the Good News, must be done freely. As a spiritual director, you are listening to the movement of the spirit in the directee. Although listening skills are involved, the central gift you rely on in this ministry is your faith that God's Spirit is alive and active in your directees. In reality, the Spirit is the director. Your faith welcomes the Spirit's wisdom and love into your very being and Her presence values you for who you are rather than for any compensation you receive. Your value lies is being the unique Spirit-led person you are. You also believe that the movement of the Spirit can be recognized and followed. Your faith empowers your directees to trust their own faith response.

The second letter comes from a writer who sees spiritual direction as a profession:

> You are a member of the profession of spiritual directors, not a volunteer. As a spiritual director, you are responsible to many: to yourself, to your directees, to other directors, to society and to God. People generally communicate value by paying for it. The courage to ask your directees for a just compensation is an exercise of your professional responsibility and one way to affirm your value. When you set a just fee, you act justly. When you set a just fee, you admit that God does not write checks to pay for room and board but rather empowers you to support yourself. In setting a just fee, you communicate to your directees how deeply you value their attentiveness to the Holy One's presence in their lives. Think about setting a sliding fee scale and offer to the poorest seekers other ways to contribute; even the poor want to be invited to give something as a recognition of their deep dignity. None of us can allow ourselves to be devalued. Furthermore, in setting a just fee, you face those attitudes and voices that help to render spiritual direction as a secondary or even unacknowledged ministry. These voices and attitudes can keep us from being full-time spiritual directors.[12]

The growth of professionalism has several roots. On the question of payment for direction, I suspect that much of the impetus has come from the Roman Catholic side. A significant number of directors are women who are either currently members of religious orders or were so in the past. The communities need money and sisters may be encouraged to earn money for their communities in spiritual direction as in the past they might have through teaching, nursing, or parish work. The religious who have returned to secular life, often in middle age, find that the religious life has given them a special gift that is best used in spiritual direction, but they also need to earn money to live. The same is true of single women who have found the fulfillment of a call to ministry in direction means that they give up a job that used to provide their livelihood.

As far as the more general issues of professionalism are concerned, I recognize the American genius for coming up with accreditation in all sorts of fields of human work and skill. Here, though, there is a sharper pressure. Recent years have seen in many of the churches a disturbing increase in litigation over instances of clergy abusing their powers as givers of pastoral care and these have resulted in large compensation payments to the plaintiffs. Several of those with whom I have spoken talk of the power of insurance corporations to determine the shape of pastoral care. Some Episcopal dioceses have produced stringent regulations limiting the number of sessions a pastor may hold with someone without seeking formal supervision. There is a real fear of abusive relationships that may lead to scandal, court cases, and large monetary awards, not to mention the damage caused to the people concerned. The most anxiety is felt and most safeguards are put in place where there is an imbalance of power between the two people in a pastoral relationship, especially when they are of different sexes.

Against that background it is understandable that Spiritual Directors International is moving towards becoming a professional body, with all that the word implies. At the time of writing the association has produced for experiment and comment a draft code of conduct with guidelines for spiritual directors. Much of the document is simply a description of good pastoral practice in any language. Some of it smacks more of the disciplines of psychotherapy and counseling than of the charism of spiritual direction. Occasional elements look like legalism. In the first section of the draft guidelines, under the heading *Spiritual Director and the Self: Personal Spirituality*, I find the order of suggestions indicative:

> Spiritual directors assume responsibility for personal growth by
>
> a) engaging in regular spiritual direction
>
> b) following personal and communal spiritual practices and disciplines.

It seems to suggest that having a spiritual director is more important than the pursuit of holiness. As T. S. Eliot wrote in *Four Quartets* of the seeker coming to pray at the parish church at Little Gidding,

> You are not here to verify,
> Instruct yourself, or inform curiosity
> Or carry report. You are here to kneel
> Where prayer has been valid.[13]

Similarly, the seeker after spiritual direction also seeks a center of holiness, "where prayer has been valid." So the primary source of any director's effectiveness has to be his or her validity as a person in relation to God.

I was once taken by surprise when a student at an Episcopal seminary asked me if I had a spiritual direction "practice," which for me conjured up images of an office suite with a receptionist and dedicated consulting room. There would be a table of fees and certificates of degrees and professional qualifications on the walls, not to mention a notice on the street door advertising my trade. Yet on second thought I recognized that I do spend about two days a week engaged with people on what we know as spiritual direction, that a large number of people use me for that purpose, and that the reason for this is presumably that they find that I am able to walk with them in a way that is helpful enough for them to come back regularly. What is more, people do give me money—not as a fee, but to help towards my expenses. So I had to ask myself whether "practice" might be an accurate description after all, even though the idea of certificates on the wall got under my skin!

Divisions over questions of training, qualification, and accreditation among leading people in the world of spiritual direction runs deep. Pressure about payments, insurance, security, professional standards, and oversight confronts a deeply held belief in spiritual direction as a response to a God-given vocation, where the gifts and skills required are seen primarily as charism. There are many directors who advertise themselves as graduates of one training program or another. Equally, there are training courses which, though they may give a certificate that someone has completed the course, at the same time give a letter making it quite clear that the completion of a course of training in no way qualifies a person to be known as a spiritual director.

In *Spiritual Direction for Every Christian* Gordon Jeff begins his chapter on training by observing, "There may be some younger people to whom others are drawn in a search for direction, but more generally we look in a director for a quality of maturity and integration that takes time to develop."[14] This recognition that "age in Christ" is vital in a director goes right back to the beginning of spiritual direction. In the late third century St. Antony of Egypt retired into the desert and for twenty years lived a hermit's life of discipline and devotion. People were attracted by his holiness to come for advice and to join him. After those twenty years he came out of his solitude to establish a religious community of hermits who accepted a common rule of life.

The earliest writings on spiritual direction were

stories and aphorisms from an oral tradition springing out of lives lived in the deserts of Syria and Egypt. The work was essentially making sense of chaotic emotions, disordered imagination, lofty aspirations and deep betrayals in the presence of God, something that concerns us all.... We read in these stories of conversations where the "good thoughts" as well as the "bad thoughts" are opened up in the presence of the charismatic elder. The wide ranging conversation helped the work of God in the whole life of the aspirant to be available to the elder before s/he responded by "speaking a word." The ministry invited the aspirant into a further engagement with and a deeper commitment to God.... The elder supported that process, offered the wisdom of experience, and was compassionate in hearing the struggle and pain, as well as receiving the joy and increasing insight.

Right from those early days until today, a tension has existed between the authentic charism and "going visible."[15]

This recognition of the need for time in which spiritual maturity may develop is echoed in the Russian Orthodox tradition. St. Seraphim of Sarov stands out as a model of the spiritual father. He spent twenty solitary years in the forest before returning to the town where he was recognized for the holiness and wisdom of his advice.

Those looking for help and counsel recognize not a technical skill but something that they sense comes from God. This is the fruit of time spent listening to God, often in long periods of contemplative prayer. So it is right that training courses should concentrate above all on helping their members to grow in Christ and to deepen their own spirituality in order to be more available to be used by the Holy Spirit in accompanying other people. There are, however, certain skills that must be learned or be developed through a course, such as the ability to listen sensitively and with discernment. In part it has to be a gift, but it can be improved by practice in training. Insights and skills from the world of psychology and counseling can form a valuable part of the syllabus. In many different ways, someone who is already being used by other people can be enabled to be a better director.

The tension between the need for inward spiritual growth and for technical skill-training is well described by one spiritual director:

> I am bothered that books about spiritual direction may draw us to the "outside" rather than help us to focus on the "inside" of the ministry of spiritual direction. No amount of others telling us "how to do it" or reflection on their experience can make up for the need for discernment in terms of our own call to this ministry. The greatest resource that a spiritual director has is his or her own commitment to that all-embracing activity that we call prayer. A second resource is receiving spiritual direction. A third resource is the experience of exercising the ministry. For some, a fourth resource, some training to provide an arena for structured reflection on the ministry and to hone skills is of great value.[16]

As someone who has received training both through my own spiritual direction and supervision and also through specific courses and events, I am strongly in favor of helping people to grow in this way. However, I share with Kenneth Leech an aversion to the idea that spiritual directors can be put through examinations and given diplomas or qualifications to practice. It simply is not like that. Repeatedly over different generations people have prayed that God would provide suitable directors. I rejoice that in our day it looks as if that prayer is beginning to be fulfilled and that increasingly the means are becoming available to help them to exercise their ministry more fruitfully.

Endnotes

1. Kenneth Leech, *The Tablet*, May 22, 1993.

2. Foster Freeman, *Spiritual Growth: An Empirical Exploration of its Meaning, Sources and Implications* (Washington, D.C.: Metropolitan Ecumenical Training Center, 1974), 9-10; 29.

3. Tilden Edwards, *Spiritual Friend* (New York: Paulist, 1980), 15,17.

4. Sandra Schneiders, "Horizons of Spiritual Direction," *Horizons* 11:100ff.

5. F. P. Harton, *The Elements of the Spiritual Life* (London: SPCK, 1932), v; 333-336.

6. Urban T. Holmes III, *Spirituality for Ministry* (San Francisco: Harper & Row, 1982), xi.

7. Martin Thornton, *The Rock and the River* (London: Hodder & Stoughton, 1965), 134.

8. Martin Thornton, *Spiritual Direction* (Cambridge, Mass.: Cowley Publications, 1987), ix; 7; 125.

9. Gordon Jeff, *Spiritual Direction for Every Christian* (London: SPCK, 1987), 3; 73-74.

10. Margaret Guenther, *Holy Listening: The Art of Spiritual Direction* (Cambridge, Mass.: Cowley Publications, 1992), 1.

11. Michael Marshall, *Church of England Newspaper*, January 12, 1996.

12. Bill Creed, "Dignity and Worth: The Question of Compensation for Spiritual Direction," *Presence: An International Journal of Spiritual Direction* 1:3.

13. T. S. Eliot, "Little Gidding," *Four Quartets* (London: Faber & Faber, 1944).

14. Jeff, *Spiritual Direction*, 74.

15. Barbara Doubtfire, *Spiritual Direction Network* 15 (February 1995).

16. *Ibid.*

Chapter 9

Spiritual Direction and Community

The life of a group in which people find the security of confidentiality and clear boundaries enables them to be open and to grow. The mutual support and challenge of such groups offer help that is similar to that of individual spiritual direction, and it is a common experience for people to learn and to grow in and through the friendships that spring up in small groups even when the group has been formed for a far different purpose. They are helped by working together under some discipline to achieve a common task.

So far we have generally thought of spiritual direction as taking place in a one-to-one meeting, but it is quite clear that Anglicans have a long tradition of helping people to grow in the Christian way through different sorts of groups. The eighteenth-century evangelical revival saw the beginning of what has become part of evangelical culture: the prayer group, with its most clearly defined form in the Methodist class meeting. Furthermore, today we have study groups, prayer groups, "cells," and several different sorts of small Christian communities. All deserve to be considered within the wider context of spiritual direction.

Family Prayers

The first group within which people grow and learn is the family. For many generations it was expected that church-going Anglicans would supplement their attendance at worship with prayers in the home. In earlier centuries the idea of family was wider than ours today: a household would consist not only of several generations of blood relations but also of servants and apprentices. Heads of families assumed responsibility not only for the religious upbringing of their own children, but also for that of the young people and older employees in their charge, as is borne out by this rubric to the catechism in prayer books of the period:

> All Fathers, Mothers, Masters and Dames shall cause their Children, Servants and Prentices (which have not learned their Catechism) to come to the Church at the time appointed and obediently to hear and be ordered by the Curate until such time as they have learned all that is here appointed.

In his life of the seventeenth-century parson George Herbert, Izaak Walton wrote of his habit of appearing

> constantly with his wife and three nieces and his whole family twice every day at the Church prayers, in the chapel which does almost adjoin to his Parsonage House. And his constant public prayers did never make him to neglect his own private devotions, nor those prayers that he thought himself bound to perform with his family, which always were a set form, and not long. Thus he made every day's sanctity a step towards that Kingdom where impurity cannot enter.[1]

Walton's biography was certainly a work of hagiography, for he was writing the life of a recognized saint. But the devotional pattern is there, even if in many cases it would not have been followed with the same diligence.

Family prayers were also a recognized part of devotion among evangelicals from the eighteenth century onwards, though the really formative innovation from that time was the system of class meetings that John Wesley introduced in his new Methodist societies. As early as 1738 Wesley organized these local societies of converts into "bands." Later the "classes" were formed; these were less selective than the bands and open to all who desired to be saved from their sins. Discipline under the lay leadership was strict. Members were expected to be at church and at the Lord's Table every week and at each of the class meetings. They were to be diligent and regular in hearing God's word, in private prayer, and in their own reading of the Bible, and to observe Friday as a day of fasting.

Both men and women served as class leaders, and Wesley required that they should "make particular inquiry" into the conduct of members in their class meetings. Attendance at these meetings was required, moreover, not as a formality but as an occasion for the renewal of spiritual oversight and fellowship and for the shared experience in the art of Christian living. There was rigorous mutual examination with testimony and confession. What is remarkable about this way of spiritual direction is not only that it took place within the context of fellowship in the group, but that it was essentially exercised by lay men and women. Ordinary people who showed that they had suitable gifts were expected to be pastors to the flock, with the minister responsible for their training and oversight. Although in some places the practice of class meetings continued late into the twentieth century, it seems that its original force tended to weaken.

Cells and Prayer Groups

Class meetings may have been peculiar to Methodism, but it is possible to see a similar purpose and certainly a similar effect in many prayer groups and home meetings. For example, an initiative of Reginald Somerset Ward's in 1937 led to an important movement in the Church of England: the creation of small prayer groups, or "cells." For some years Ward had been acutely aware of the needs and deficiencies of the young clergymen he met in his work in different parts of the country and he shared this anxiety with Arthur Langford Jones, an experienced spiritual director who died in 1937, and Leslie Owen, principal of the theological college at Lincoln and later Bishop of Lincoln. In January 1937 Somerset Ward, Lumsden Barkway, Edmund Morgan, and Leslie Owen met for the first time for mutual fellowship and prayer, and this first cell group continued to meet about twice a year. Several years later Ward wrote an essay entitled "Fellowship in the Gospel" where he presented both the theory underlying the cell and the way it worked. Although he resisted strongly any organization of cells as counter to their basic philosophy, he also recognized the need for some guidance at a time when the idea was spreading and new groups were being formed, often at the initiative of members of the first cell.

He began by recognizing that

> a highly organised Church is always open to certain dangers and diseases. Chief among these dangers is the replacement of deep spiritual vigour by surface activity. One way this danger has been met has always been by movements from within the Church, by the efforts of small collections of individuals under divine inspiration. The origin is the arousing by God of anxiety in a few individuals concerning some aspect of the Church's

work. In most cases the attempt to meet this anxiety has taken the form of committees, conferences or councils. There remains doubt as to whether the stirring of the Holy Spirit manifest in this anxiety can be met completely by these forms of expression.

Working from the natural basic unit of creation, the atom, Ward suggested that a small number of individuals

so united by love and faith and the consciousness of the anxiety of the Holy Ghost that they cohered in one common purpose and ideals bind themselves to His service as a living atom.

The "Fellowship in the Gospel" was a body of individuals who yielded themselves to the power of the Holy Spirit. In contrast to a committee, which is primarily concerned with the form of its activity, the fellowship was concerned with its life. That was its purpose: to live, to receive its life from God, and to offer its life for God's use. The coherence of the "electrons"— to use Somerset Ward's image—that compose this atom, the individuals united in fellowship, is due to a twofold relationship. On the one side, there is a mutual, intentional, and far-reaching dependence on God; on the other, a sincere desire to learn from and cooperate with one's fellow Christians. Thus each member of the cell must have an intense desire to be used by God and a readiness to accept the cost.

Part of this cost was the very high priority expected to be given to the regular meetings, which could last anywere from twenty-four to forty hours. There was to be no attempt to produce any organization or program of future action. "The members of the Fellowship," Ward wrote, "must not come to it heavy with ideas, but heavy with the desire that God may have yet one more instrument to use in this world." Publicity is to be avoided: "the meeting is addressed to God rather than to man." The two essentials are daily prayer for each member and observing the dates and times of meetings.

The suggested timetable for meetings provided for a balance between time spent in prayer together and individually, time spent in discussion, and time spent in recreation, all leading to the formulation of a record of the meeting and any conclusions to be offered at a final eucharist. Leadership of each meeting was to be chosen by lot and, true to the non-hierarchical nature of the fellowship, had authority only to keep track of the time, open the discussions, and write up the minutes of the session.

In a letter to E. R. Morgan following the first meeting Somerset Ward wrote:

> I feel it is of the character of a cell that it grows rather than is shaped, and that anything that emerges from it so far from being a duty will be an urgent desire. I do not think it is a standard of prayer that is required, but an oblation, a desire for God to have us in all our poverty.

It is clear from the records that as well as dealing with the subject under discussion, members were keenly aware of the way the life of the group shaped their own lives, as Ward wrote in 1944: "We need to remind ourselves daily of the necessity of confronting and conquering scepticism in ourselves." In a letter to Lumsden Barkway he also spoke of "the warmth of unity" he experienced in the chapel, that love and affection that he felt lay at the heart of all human relationships. He wrote too of the effect upon himself and more particularly on his style as a director:

I have felt astonishingly fortified in my work since and have gained immensely from the simplicity of effort the cell taught us, so that, instead of trying to say everything I can in direction, I try to say one thing.

In his summary of a later meeting there is the interesting note:

We cannot choose the ground on which to fight the Lord's battles, but it is possible to fight on the wrong ground if there is no unitive prayer and wise, experienced direction at a time when a man's devotional vocabulary needs to be purged of so many words in the great manuals.[2]

In her biography of Robert Runcie, Margaret Duggan writes of the archbishop's involvement in the group. It was while he was principal of Cuddesdon Theological College that Runcie joined.

What few people knew was that, since the summer of 1963, he had been a member of 'the Cell', a tiny group of Christians who supported each other in prayer and had an unseen influence on the theological colleges. The Cell had first been gathered in 1937 by Somerset Ward, one of the unsung saints among spiritual directors, who had invited Leslie Owen, Lumsden Barkway and E. R. Morgan (all future bishops), together with the Provost of Newcastle, J. N. Bateman-Champain, to join him in two days of prayer and discussion. At the next meeting they added the Bishop of Knaresborough, P. F. D. Labilliere, and in 1942 they were joined by Eric Abbott (subsequently Dean of Westminster) who, as Somerset Ward aged, became the pivot of the group.

In the early years there were never more than six members, and new ones joined only when the older ones died or became too elderly to attend the meetings regularly....The Cell met (and continues to meet) approximately every nine months, usually from a Friday afternoon to a Sunday morning. The strictly disciplined program was divided between prayer and discussion, the daily offices, civilised meals, and silence. Attendance at the meetings was obligatory and that attendance, together with praying for each other every day, were the only rules they all had to keep.

The subject for each meeting was selected after a period of prayer, followed by discussion and more prayer. At [Runcie's] first meeting it was "How is the contemporary crisis in Western society affecting the young priest in his prayers and his affections?"[3]

For Runcie the importance of these meetings increased over the years and he encouraged his students to form cells for themselves, as has happened in other theological colleges like King's College, London, and Salisbury. Several of these fellowships still continue to meet. Relationships within the cells need to be based on natural friendship, and from the start it was important that members were able to trust and appreciate one another. Runcie has spoken of being invited to meetings at which the members celebrate twenty-five years together. He elaborated his own experience of the value of members' honesty towards each other, turning to one another for support in decisions that have to be made and events that happen in their lives and ministries. The successors to the original cell share the same "anxiety" that occasioned its foundation in the first place, namely the training of young clergy. Perhaps there is a greater emphasis than earlier on the mutual help that members give each other. Alongside the influence of Somerset Ward there has also been the increasing influence of the teaching of Gilbert Shaw and his insistence on what he called "the great tradition," which is the common mystical tradition of both eastern and western Christians.

The tradition of Christians praying together with one another goes back to the gospels and Jesus' saying, "Wherever two or three are met together in my name, there am I in the midst of them." Prayer groups of many different kinds feature large in the landscape of Anglicanism today. There are the ecumenical network of Julian meetings, named after Julian of Norwich and given to contemplative prayer, the prayer groups that arise out of Cursillo, and the widespread parish and fellowship groups meeting in people's homes. One interesting variation on this theme began with Evelyn Underhill and her leadership of a group that came to be known as the Fellowship of St. Faith, which served a wide circle of people of all ages looking for depth of spirituality and a comprehensible faith. After Underhill's death her friend Agatha Norman, who had assisted her with prayer groups and retreats, continued to develop the prayer groups from her home in Sussex until Eric Abbott, newly appointed dean of King's College, London, invited her to become tutor for women theological students there. Under Norman's leadership this became the largest group of such students in the country, many of them going on to positions of influence and responsibility. She continued the work with prayer groups, schools of prayer, and retreats at Pleshey. At first St. Paul's Knightsbridge provided a base for her group and later Westminster Abbey, where Eric Abbott was by then dean.

After her retirement Agatha Norman lived in an apartment in the precincts at Canterbury, starting prayer groups there and continuing to lead retreats. In his funeral sermon Canon Frank Telfer said of her:

> Whatever experience of God it was that Agatha had at the age of six, it determined the context of the rest of her life. Her conversion (for so she spoke of it) was a true gift of grace, for it freed her and sustained her. She was one of the most mature adults that I have ever met, both realistic and full of faith.

> If the ethos of the Fellowship of St. Faith was Evelyn Underhill, the organization and execution were distinctively Agatha's. But it was much more than administrative efficiency, for with her prayer and life walked together....Everyone will have distinctive and different memories to treasure. She would bend her mind to your problem with total attention and require total attention when she spoke: "There are some things I wish you to hear." Her advice was far-reaching and sound, full of wisdom and understanding.[4]

Group Spiritual Direction

As well as these instances where spiritual direction takes place almost incidentally among people who have met for a different, if related, purpose, a growing number of people are doing spiritual direction together in the context of a group. Rose Mary Dougherty gives an insightful description of the approach followed at the Shalem Institute in Washington, D. C., with its strongly ecumenical base. From her long experience as a director and as one who has provided direction in the setting of a group, she offers practical advice on the choice of participants, on the length and frequency of meetings, and on the use of facilitators. Throughout her book the theological rationale for group direction is clear:

Spiritual community both fosters and demands the asceticism of radical love, a love that we can only pray for and be open to receiving. It is characterized by a singlemindedness, a love of God that encompasses and directs our love of others. It is a love that we gradually grow into and we pray for an attitude of intercessory prayer.

It is against this background of prayerful openness to God and to the other people in the group that she outlines the process that the groups follow:

Group direction is grounded in Mystery. We use a very simple process which honors and supports the grounding: silence, the sharing of a participant, silence, response from the group, silence. We repeat this process until all individuals have had time for their sharing and response from the group. We add a few minutes at the end to reflect on our time together. Prayerful silence nurtures discernment in group spiritual direction, just as it does in one-to-one spiritual direction.... The attitude of intercessory prayer is nurtured in settings like group spiritual direction. Here people are present to God for others in the group. Here, as participants in group spiritual direction attest, they are gifted by the praying presence of others.

In keeping with the ethos of the Shalem Institute, with its recognition of the truth and value of contemplative prayer, Dougherty gives space to this element within the work of a group.

Group spiritual direction can be a form of contemplative prayer. It is a communal and individual offering to God of time together, asking to assist one another in seeing "what is." There is a vulnerability involved in group spiritual direction. We are asked to share our spiritual hearts with others and be open to receiving what they offer of themselves. As we come in touch with the Mystery of God in the depths of our being, and that of others in the group, we come in contact with the "heart of the world" with whom we share this Mystery.[5]

How effective and rewarding this kind of group work can be I know from several years of experience in a group of people whose prayer follows the contemplative way. The pattern has developed of a meeting twice a year, with up to ten of us spending two nights away in a retreat house. An evening, one whole day, and the next morning provide the space for a balanced program of periods of silent prayer, often together in the same place; for careful sharing of the prayer and of our own lives; for the eucharist and other formal times of prayer; and also for informal times of simply being together, walking and talking.

As Rose Mary Dougherty makes clear, this sort of meeting requires a certain basis in shared assumptions and expectations as well as an accepted discipline. It requires that people be aware of the main reasons why they and the others are there in the first place, as well as an agreed-upon structure for discussions that allows individuals the time and the attention to be heard without interruption. Group spiritual direction's basis in intercession and attitudes of mutual prayer are aspects that ideally are present from the start, but that will grow to be increasingly vital in the group's life. We are a gathering of men and women, each with his or her own insight into prayer and each involved in a very active life and ministry, whether as clergy or lay people. It has been very helpful to have a consultant with us, a religious sister who has been led a long way along the road of contemplative prayer.

The effect of this mutual accompanying, a form of group direction, has been much valued by people taking part. They speak of the importance of the protected time and space; of the sense of affirmation and encouragement offered by the insights given by the others; and of the gifts in the stories of different people, which deepen an awareness of the breadth of Christian experience.

Servants of Christ the King

Now over fifty years old, the movement called Servants of Christ the King has clear affinities with prayer cells but also has distinctive characteristics of its own. It is a fellowship of small groups, called companies, that are mostly comprised of lay people who are seeking to model their lives on the example and teachings of Christ. Originated by a priest in the Church of England called Roger Lloyd, it began within the Anglican Communion but has been open to all Christians since 1964.

In his book *An Adventure in Discipleship* Lloyd describes how, at a clergy conference, he and three other priests came together and agreed, "We needed some instrument more radical and much more spiritually basic than anything we could see coming out of that conference." They recognized there was no instrument available at that time to meet the church's urgent need if it was to bring the Gospel to all the people. Their reading of the Bible seemed to point towards a series of small groups of dedicated Christians who would work out their discipleship together and "by waiting upon God become exceedingly close-knit communities in Christ."

The vocation of the SCK today is "to be the servants of Christ the King in the world" in the hope that society will find its way back to God. Its approach and purpose are summarized in the membership card:

We, the Servants of Christ the King, wait upon God
In order to seek his will
We keep silence in company
We listen to each other in turn
We look for a common concern
In our work for his kingdom
Always expecting unanimous agreement
Before taking major decisions.

Centered in its concern for the gospel and the coming of God's kingdom, the SCK supports a varied program of projects in evangelism and pastoral care.

For its first twelve years, the Servants of Christ the King grew without publicity. Much as with the cells, the quality of hiddenness was thought to be critical. Later the decision was made to go public and Lloyd's book was one of the results. A second close connection with the prayer cells lies in the belief that common decisions are only to be reached through a process of silent prayer and discernment, waiting upon God.

What about the effect that the life of the groups has on their members? Roger Lloyd writes movingly of this influence as one of the positive achievements of the movement:

I should place very high on the list what under God it has done for its individual members. There is no question about it. People of all kinds and ages, but above all the young, who spend a number of years in one of our companies, who subject themselves faithfully to its disciplines, do grow up in Christ in the most astonishing way. It seems to keep them quick and eager, courteous and loving, and to sharpen and temper all the native spiritual faculties they had to begin with.[6]

In the end, whether it is in the more tightly structured experience of a prayer cell, or in a Methodist class, or in the open relationship of a group of friends meeting in one another's homes, it is clear that spiritual direction takes place in the openness of people to one another and to the Holy Spirit. It is also true that growth in Christ may turn out to be the outcome rather than the stated purpose of the group. Often it is when Christians are working together at some depth for a particular purpose that they find themselves challenged as to their own discipleship and look to others for the kind of help that exists within the body of Christ.

Endnotes

1. Quoted in More and Cross, *Anglicanism*, 734.

2. MS 2946 in Lambeth Palace Library.

3. Margaret Duggan, *Runcie, The Making of an Archbishop* (London: Hodder & Stoughton, 1983), 134ff.

4. Frank Telfer, sermon preached at Canterbury Cathedral, Canterbury, 1989.

5. Rose Mary Dougherty, SSND, *Group Spiritual Direction: Community for Discernment* (New York: Paulist, 1995), 14; 35; 88; 75.

6. Roger Lloyd, *An Adventure in Discipleship* (London: Longmans Green, 1953), 26.

Chapter 10

Afterword

A s I consider all these varied examples of people who stand out in the Anglican church's story as guides and counselors in matters of the spirit and the Christian life, I find that there are certain characteristics that many of them share. For one, religion is not something to make a person feel better or to give spiritual excitement; religion is the heart of living a good life in relation to God and to other human beings. Humane is a word that springs to mind to describe this tradition. Many of the people we have looked to expressed love, kindliness, and real compassion for those who came to them. The language they use is one of healing and of growth, rather than of the law court—judgment, condemnation, and punishment. Not that these elements are absent, for few of the people we have looked at could be called vague or soft-hearted. But the pastoral roots of the Anglican tradition of spiritual direction mean that its practitioners are counselors, confessors, and physicians of the soul, not judges. There is warmth and a lightness of touch.

Allied with this is the classic Anglican sense of moderation. The Anglican sensibility does not favor extremes; much of its counsel advises the common sense way. It endorses real religion but draws away from excessive religiosity. Its prayers may be deep, but they are simple, unfussy. Instead of over-pious scruples it values straightforward advice about everyday living. The Anglican way of spiritual direction has usually been local, low key, and practical.

It may sound contradictory, but I suspect that many of the people we have surveyed would have shrunk from the label of spiritual director. It is only fairly recently that the title has become respectable in our church; remember that Pusey, a wise and holy giver of spiritual counsel, refused to use it. I wonder whether this is because the Anglican tradition of authority resting in the Bible, the church tradition, and human, God-given reason has given us a very strong respect for the individual's freedom and right to make his or her own decisions.

Also very much in the Anglican ethos is the wide variety of styles and approaches to spiritual direction. Clearly there is no one way to do it. Technical skills are less respected than a closeness to God and a generosity of spirit. There is even a broad diversity in understanding what is actually meant by spiritual direction, all the way from two Christian friends walking together to the practice of a professionally qualified person. The latter, however, is likely to be more acceptable in America than on the other side of the Atlantic; in Britain greater emphasis is placed on the director as a gifted amateur. Similarly, in the United States there is much greater overlap with counseling and psychotherapy, nor can I see moves towards anything like a professional body on the lines of Spiritual Directors International in England.

Researching this book has meant meeting people who are active in this ministry and reading a range of different books by writers past and present. It has left me—and I hope it has left you—with the heartening sense that in Anglicanism can be found a living and valid expression of Christian pastoring that is both true to our heritage and at the same time open to dialogue and exchange with what is best in other Christian traditions. I look forward to our growing in maturity, giving full value to our God-given diversity and open to the changes that growth in Christ brings.